Armistead Churchill Gordon

Congressional Currency

An Outline of the Federal Money System

Armistead Churchill Gordon

Congressional Currency
An Outline of the Federal Money System

ISBN/EAN: 9783337232771

Printed in Europe, USA, Canada, Australia, Japan

Cover: Foto ©Suzi / pixelio.de

More available books at **www.hansebooks.com**

CONGRESSIONAL CURRENCY

AN OUTLINE OF THE FEDERAL
MONEY SYSTEM

BY

ARMISTEAD C. GORDON

" The best thing undeniably that a Government can
do with the Money Market is to let it take care of itself."
WALTER BAGEHOT, *Lombard Street*, Chap. IV.

G. P. PUTNAM'S SONS

NEW YORK   LONDON
27 WEST TWENTY-THIRD STREET   24 BEDFORD STREET, STRAND
The Knickerbocker Press
1895

"The value of the dollar of account ought not to depend upon an accidental majority : it should represent invariably a certain weight and fineness of the precious metals, and Congress should have nothing to do with it except to see that the makers of a credit currency redeem their promises in coin or go out of business. That is the duty of the government, and there its duty ends."

H. W. RICHARDSON.

PREFACE.

It is the object of these chapters to present within a brief compass and with as little technicality as possible an outline of the genesis, growth, and condition of the existing currency system of the United States, a short account of each of the various kinds of "money" or circulating medium now in use, and a consecutive statement of the most conspicuous or important acts of legislation in connection therewith, concluding with a sketch of the judicial interpretation which such legislation has received at the hands of the Supreme Court. To have sought to trace in detail the records of monetary events, and to narrate the financial history of the government from its foundation, might have been both profitable and pertinent to the subject in hand; but, for the sake of brevity, the scope of this work has been so limited

as not only to exclude such an historical re-
trospect except in the most cursory manner,
but no less a discussion of those intimate
relations borne to finance and currency by
trade and commerce. The simple purpose
of the book is to outline the Federal money
system as it exists to-day, and to sketch
the legislation by the Congress in regard
to money and currency during that period
of the history of the United States
embraced between the year 1861 and the
present time; a period, which may be
conveniently described as consisting of two
divisions; one in which the Congress has,
in a comparative degree, only, controlled
by its enactments the circulating medium,
beginning with the greenback legislation,
and ending with the imposition of the ten
per cent. tax on State bank issues ; and the
other, in which the currency of the country
has been made and managed with an iron
hand by the National Legislature, beginning
with the date of the last-named enactment,
and continuing up to the present time.

As an appropriate part of such a sketch,
the machinery and methods through which

this congressional control is exerted and directed are first given in brief chapters on the United States Treasury, the Sub-Treasury, the National Banking Associations, the Clearing-Houses, and the Public Debt and Gold Reserve.

For the double purpose of verifying the statements of facts presented, and of possibly inciting others to the further investigation of a subject which should be familiar, in degree, at least to every American citizen, frequent citations of authorities have been made

STAUNTON, VA.,
Sept. 25, 1895.

CONTENTS.

		PAGE
I.	INTRODUCTORY	1
II.	THE UNITED STATES TREASURY DEPARTMENT	24
III.	THE INDEPENDENT TREASURY OR SUB-TREASURY OF THE UNITED STATES .	37
IV.	THE NATIONAL BANKING ASSOCIATIONS .	56
V.	THE CLEARING-HOUSE ASSOCIATIONS	68
VI.	THE PUBLIC DEBT AND THE GOLD RESERVE	83
VII.	GOLD COINS ; THE SILVER DOLLAR ; AND SUBSIDIARY COINAGE .	96
VIII.	UNITED STATES NOTES, OR "GREENBACKS" ; POSTAL CURRENCY, AND FRACTIONAL CURRENCY .	125
IX.	NATIONAL BANK NOTES . .	151
X.	GOLD CERTIFICATES, SILVER CERTIFICATES, TREASURY NOTES OF 1890, AND CURRENCY CERTIFICATES . .	173
XI.	JUDICIAL INTERPRETATION OF CURRENCY LEGISLATION . .	190
XII.	CONCLUSION .	204
INDEX . .		229

CONGRESSIONAL CURRENCY:

AN OUTLINE OF THE FEDERAL MONEY SYSTEM.

I.

INTRODUCTORY.

THE monetary transactions of the government and of the people of the United States are conducted with money bearing the government's stamp of weight and fineness, and with paper currency prepared and furnished by the government, all emanating from the Treasury Department at Washington, under and by virtue of acts of the Congress, either directly, as in case of the greenbacks, the gold and silver certificates, the currency certificates and the Treasury notes of 1890; or indirectly, as in the case of the national bank notes, which are issued under statutory restrictions and limitations, and are secured by government bonds.

The currency circulation is accurately divisible into two classes, viz. : money, which includes gold coins, the standard silver dollar, and subsidiary coins; and currency proper,[1] which consists of greenbacks, national bank notes, gold certificates, silver certificates and Treasury or coin notes. Thus there are nine kinds of circulating medium in the United States, having the stamp and approval and backed by the credit of the government.   In times of panic and financial crisis, under our peculiar system even these nine kinds of money have proved insufficient, and resort has been had in the cities of the United States to a tenth species of currency, not emanating, however, from the Congress, nor recognized by it, but serving a potential and valuable purpose at such periods, viz. : the clearing-house certificates.

Of the results of the War between the States, which begun in 1861 and ended in

---

[1] Webster's *Works*, vol. iv., p. 271.

1865, the ultimate settlement of the doctrine of secession in the negative, and the
emancipation and enfranchisement of the
Southern slaves, if apparently the most
conspicuous at its close, were not the most
important and far reaching in their conse-
quences upon the future welfare of the
American people. "An indissoluble Union
of indestructible States " has long been the
creed of patriotic Americans, North and
South ; and the " Negro Question " has of
late years settled itself to the general satisfaction of the whole country. But the bur-
den of financial legislation resulting from
the War lies heavily upon the people of the
United States thirty years after the War's
end.

As tremendous in its significance as it
was rapid in its consummation, was the
irresistible aggregation, under the exigent
stress of conflict, into the hands of the Congress of the United States, within a period
of some four or five years, of all the financial and currency forces of the country,
with the stupendous powers and capabili-
ties for good and evil which the possession

and control of those forces necessarily im-
ply. Down through the story of the government, from its foundation to the final
establishment of the Sub-Treasury system,
proposed under Jackson and accomplished
under Van Buren, had run like a red thread
the line of politico-economic controversy
over the currency. Hamilton, in his mas-
terly " Report on a National Bank," [1] had in
1790, not only prefigured and advocated a
system of finance which the political party
to which he belonged, and its legitimate
successors, adopted as a conspicuous part of
their political creed, but he had foreshadowed the enunciation of that "sovereignty
of the federal government within its specified bounds" on which the United States
Supreme Court rested its last and far-reaching legal-tender decision in 1884. Hamilton's great antagonist, Thomas Jefferson, on
the other hand, had instilled into the minds
of his party followers that the constitutional provision for the laying of the federal
taxes was the *power*, and the general welfare the *purpose* for which the power was

---

[1] *Reports on the Finances*, vol. I, p. 54.

to be exercised; and had antagonized the establishment of a national bank as unnecessary and unauthorized.

The organization of the first Bank of the United States had aroused a fierce contest between Federalists and Republicans, the latter holding it to be in violation of the Constitution; but in 1815 the Republican party had favored the recharter of the Bank, its leaders asserting that the Bank's continued existence would tend to check the increase of the state banks and curtail their undesirable paper circulation. In 1817 the second Bank of the United States had gone into effect, and some ten years later, when Jackson began his onslaught upon it which culminated in the removal of the government's deposits and the subsequent expiration of its charter by limitation, the Democratic party had again returned to its first love, and espoused the cause of opposition to a national bank.

The new Constitution of the United States, adopted in 1789 by a convention from which the state of Rhode Island had absented itself on account of its unwillingness to submit its right of "independent issue" of paper money [1] had prohibited the emission by the state governments of bills of credit, and had provided that the states might make nothing but gold and silver a legal tender in payment of debt; while, in the framing of the Constitution, which gave the general government, through the Congress, the power to coin money and regulate the value thereof, a proposition to permit the Congress itself to emit bills of credit had received only two votes.[2]

At its first session under the new Constitution, the Congress had declared that only coin should be received into the Treasury in payment of the public dues; and in all the several subsequent controversies extending through a large part of the early history of the country over "hard money," the national bank question, and the Independent Treasury, the right of the Congress to make anything but gold and silver a legal tender for debt had never been practically asserted by the enactment of any

---

[1] F. A. Walker, *Money*, p. 316.
[2] J. K. Upton, *Money in Politics*, chap. viii.

law. The federal government, although
lending its aid and influence to the two
national banks of the United States in succession, had at no time undertaken, even
when issuing its obligations of indebted-
ness in the shape of interest-bearing Treasury notes, to lay its "heavy and unsteady
hand" upon the circulating medium of the
country to the exclusion of all other currency than that provided by itself; even
though such eminent party leaders and
statesmen as Alexander J. Dallas and John
C. Calhoun had maintained the position
that the Constitution gave the Congress
the exclusive power to regulate the currency of the United States.[1]

So thoroughly had the disapprobation
of the government's associating itself, even
indirectly, with the conduct of banks and
banking become ingrained in the public
mind, that even as late as 1861, when a
new party, maintaining many of the views
of Hamilton and his school of politics and
social economy, was in the ascendancy, "a

[1] W. D. Dabney, "Evolution of Paper Money," *Reports
Virginia State Bar Association*, vol. vii, p. 187.

majority of the people," says an eminent authority, " would have thought the establishment of a third United States Bank dangerous and of doubtful constitutionality." [1]   And yet, two years later, in the midst of war, the Congress of the United States established a system of national banks which the same writer says was "infinitely more powerful than the Bank which waged an almost equal war with Jackson."

The prelude to this legislation had been the issuing in the year prior thereto by the Congress, under the assumption by it of the existence of a constitutional right to exercise any power necessary to carrying on war [2] of a tremendous volume of legal-tender Treasury notes; and the not inappropriate sequence upon the national bank legislation was the prompt imposition of a tax upon state bank issues, which was rendered prohibitive in its character so soon as the original act imposing the tax re-

---

[1] Charles F. Dunbar, *The Theory and History of Banking*, chap. ix.

[2] Judge R. W. Hughes, *The Currency Question*, p. 183.

sulted in giving the information to the government how the death-blow could be most surely and safely struck. The destruction of the state bank currency resulted in the government's paper becoming the sole occupant of the currency field.

All of this centralizing legislation was, if not promptly, at least finally and unequivocally sustained by the supreme judicial tribunal of the country; though in one memorable instance, which showed that the Congress knew how both to grasp power and to wield it, the support rendered by that tribunal was under stress of compulsion. In December, 1869, the Supreme Court of the United States decided against the constitutionality of the legal-tender acts, and in the March following a vacancy occurred by the resignation of one of the justices constituting the majority. The Congress shortly theretofore, and while the case was pending before the court, had created an additional justiceship; and the Senate, carrying out the legal-tender programme to its conclusion, gave

the President to understand that no ap-
pointees to these two vacancies on the
Supreme bench would be confirmed who
were unfavorable to the legal-tender quality
of the greenback. In consequence, two justices were appointed whose views on the
question, while not "judicially pronounced,
were supposed to have been well understood by the appointing power, and to
have furnished the controlling reason for
their selection."[1]   These two newly appointed judges in December, 1870, so
changed the complexion of the court on
this question as to reverse the decision
rendered the year before, and to fix upon
the statute book as valid and constitutional the legal-tender act of February 25,
1862.[2]

The constitutional inhibition against the
states making any other thing than gold
and silver legal tender, and the no less
conspicuous omission from that instrument

[1] Dabney, " Evolution of Paper Money," *7th Virginia
Bar Association Reports.*

[2] Wilson, *Congressional Government,* 10th ed., p. 38 ; Upton, *Money in Politics,* p. 160 ; Speech of Hon. Thomas F.
Bayard in U. S. Senate, January 27, 1880.

of any provision in any of its clauses re-
lating to the finances, giving the Congress
the power to do so, was met by the Supreme Court, in the Legal Tender decisions
in 1870, with the assertion of certain implied powers of the government under the
Constitution, necessary in time of war.
But the post-bellum aggressions of the
Congress upon the currency have been no
less emphatically sustained by that high
tribunal ; for when, in March, 1884, nearly
nineteen years after the War ended, the
question again came before it in another
form, arising out of the act of 1878, which
directed that the greenbacks when redeemed should be reissued,[1] the Supreme
Court once more declared the right of the
government to make the Congress paper
promises of payment a legal tender for
debt, and went much further than in 1870
in establishing this decision upon the alleged incidental powers of sovereignty existing under the Constitution in the National
government, inherent therein and implied
as necessary to the due exercise of such

---

[1] Act, May 31, 1878.

sovereignty.[1] In the last-named case, the
question arose upon the legal-tender capacity of a war greenback when reissued
under act of the Congress in time of peace.
The result of the court's decision was so
satisfactory to the Congress, that in 1890
that body had no hesitation in giving the
legal-tender feature to the Treasury notes,
authorized by the Sherman act of that
year to be issued against accumulations of
silver bullion in the vaults of the Treasury.

The inevitable tendencies, resulting from
that subordination of state to Federal authority at every open and unguarded point,
which has been so characteristic of the general government's legislation and administration since the beginning of the Civil War
are nowhere more clearly or strikingly
reflected than in the enactments of the
Congress with reference to the currency
from 1861 up to the present time, and in
the interpretation of the most conspicuous
of these enactments by the Supreme Court
of the United States.[2]

---

[1] Juilliard *vs.* Greenman ; 110 U. S. Reports, 421.
[2] See post., ch. xi.

Yet with the power of controlling the currency, the knowledge and capacity neces. sary thereto seem in repeated instances to have been greatly wanting. Whether this is due to the fact that the work of the Congress is done through committees; that the committees which raise the revenues for the administration of government are not those which expend it; that there is no direct responsibility of the administrative financial officers of the government to the legislative body; and that interchange of opinions between the Secretary of the Treas. ury and the Congress is only contemplated in law to be made by written communica. tion, the results flowing from the financial legislation of the United States Congress have excited the astonishment of the most enlightened men of other countries. A distinguished English statesman and his- torian, who has made a profound study of our governmental system in all its relations, has conspicuously commented upon the fact that our own people have become "so puz- zled by a financial policy varying from year to year, and controlled by no responsible leaders, as to feel diminished interest in congressional discussions and diminished confidence in Congress." [1]

In this same connection may be quoted appropriately the statement of Mr. Woodrow Wilson, a recognized and distinguished authority, in his work on *Congressional Government,* that "the noteworthy fact that even the most thorough debates in Congress fail to awaken any genuine or active interest in the minds of the people has had its most striking illustrations in the course of our financial legislation ; for, though the discussions that have taken place in Congress have been so frequent, so protracted and so thorough, engrossing so large a part of the time of the House on their every recurrence, they seem, in almost every instance, to have made scarcely any impression at all upon the public mind. The Coinage act of 1873, by which silver was demonetized, had been before the country many years ere it reached adoption, having been time and again considered by

---

[1] James Bryce, *The American Commonwealth,* 2d ed., vol. i., p. 177.

committees of Congress, time and again printed and discussed in one shape or another, and having finally gained acceptance by sheer persistence and importunity. The Resumption act of 1875, too, had a like career of repeated considerations by committees, repeated printings, and a full discussion by Congress; and yet when the Bland silver bill of 1878 was on its way through the mills of legislation, some of the most prominent newspapers of the country declared with confidence that the Resumption act had been passed inconsiderately and in haste, almost secretly, indeed, and several members of Congress had previously complained that the demonetization scheme of 1873 had been pushed surreptitiously through the course of its passage, Congress having been tricked into accepting it, doing it scarcely knew what." [1]

" The financial policy," which has been alluded to as so uncertain as to be puzzling to the people at large, has, as stated by Mr. Wilson, most conspicuously assumed

---

[1] *Congressional Government*, 10th ed., p. 184.

that feature in the legislation immediately affecting the currency. Amendment has followed enactment, and repeal has followed amendment in quick succession. Currency measures, that have passed the House and been rejected by the Senate, have, in the brief course of events, been taken up and passed by the Senate to be in turn rejected by the House. Though consistently and unyieldingly assuming and asserting its undivided right of regulating and controlling currency issues, the Congress has reached its ends through devious and tortuous ways, and with legislation that has in nearly every important instance been in the nature of a compromise to tide over some imminent emergency, or a makeshift to prevent some threatening disaster. Party politics have played a conspicuous part in much of this confused legislation; and known and recognized principles of finance, and tried and conceded natural laws affecting money and currency have been whistled down the wind for the purpose of gaining partisan advantage. The possible future enactment into laws of certain financial theories has governed the admission of territories of the Union into the sisterhood of states ; and even the best informed and most experienced financiers on the floor of either house of the Congress have undoubtedly been influenced by "a profound respect for that unknown quantity, the floating vote." The balance of power, credited rightly or wrongly to some particular body of voters, has more than once moulded the financial opinion of the most distinguished Senators and Representatives.[1]

The connection between those who control and direct in private business the money and currency of the country, and the government of the United States, if not apparent on the surface, has in reality assumed a phase that would have startled the ante-bellum antagonists of a national bank; and the purposes of the Independent Treasury, created and organized with the design of getting the government out of the business of dealing in money and

---

[1] "The Future of Resumption," *North Am. Review* for August, 1879. "Should the Government Retire from Banking?" *The Forum*, Feb., 1895.

currency, have been, under congressional influences and administrative tendencies, enlarged and perverted to the erection and maintenance of a United States government bank of issue. This bank of issue is compelled to the necessity of carrying, as an essential incident to its business of banking, a gold reserve, which was actually never authorized by law, yet whose continued existence at an arbitrary figure has come almost to mean, in popular estimation, the solvency of the government itself. If there were no bank issue business done by the government, there would be no need of a "free gold" reserve; but it is because the Congress has by legislation created and put into circulation, and has by additional legislation sought to continue in circulation more than $500,000,000 of legal-tender greenbacks and Sherman Treasury notes, which are redeemable in gold by the Treasury,[1] that a gold reserve must be kept for such redemption. If the government had never gone into the bank issue business, and the Independent Treasury

---

[1] Act, March 18, 1869.   Act, July 14, 1890.

had remained limited and restricted to its original object of providing safe and convenient places for the receipt and disbursement of the government's revenues, the continued maintenance of the one hundred million dollars of free gold, first accumulated under the administration of Secretary Sherman, prior to 1879, with a view to the going into effect in that year of the Resumption act, would not, in the nature of things, have been necessary; and the Federal Treasury would have been saved the repeated and persistent "runs" that have been made upon it by every European nation which has found it desirable to increase its stock of gold, and by the gold brokers of America, who have found it profitable, when the rates of foreign exchange warranted it, to ship gold to other countries. It is one of the elementary principles of banking that banks of issue must keep a coin reserve; and when the United States makes its issues payable in gold, it must, like other banks, keep a reserve of that coin in which its notes are redeemable.

The Congress, the Supreme Court, and the several national administrations have co-operated with an ultimately certain, if at times unsteady, gravitation towards permanently maintaining the federal control of the currency, regardless of laws that are "higher, simpler, and far safer" than any the Congress can enact or the administration put into execution, and which "mock the futile efforts of those who try to overrule them."

A conspicuous instance of the confirmation, through subsequent legislation by the Congress, of acts unauthorized in law to be done by the Secretary of the Treasury, and yet done by him in the exercise of an assumed discretion nowhere distinctly conferred, may be found in Secretary Sherman's arbitrary construction that the requirements of the act of March 18, 1869, "to strengthen the public credit," and of the Resumption act of 1875, for the redemption of legal tenders in "coin," meant that they should be redeemed exclusively in gold; a policy steadfastly pursued by the government, without warrant of law, however sound financially, from 1879 up to the present time, and only at last indirectly confirmed and further authorized, after a lapse of eleven years, in the Sherman act of 1890, which provides for the redemption of the legal-tender Treasury notes issued thereunder in gold or silver coin, at the Secretary of the Treasury's discretion. [1]

A like instance is to be found in the establishment under the same act and by authority of the same Secretary, of the arbitrarily fixed "gold reserve," which was nowhere authorized by law until the passage of the act of July 12, 1882, wherein it was recognized in the provision that the reissuing of the gold certificates should be suspended "whenever the amount of gold coin and gold bullion in the Treasury reserved for the redemption of United States notes falls below one hundred millions of dollars." [2]

No less frequently, however, with an un-

---

[1] "The Future of Resumption," *North Amer. Review* for August, 1879.

[2] § 12.

certainty as to the matters of financial detail and administration, but with no relaxation of the grasp of its " heavy and unsteady hand," the Congress has illustrated the varying and puzzling policy of which Mr. Bryce speaks, in flouting the efforts of executive officers of its own party to carry out the currency and finance laws as provided ; or has steadily antagonized the attitude assumed with reference to fiscal matters by a chief executive of its party creed.

The heterogeneous and confused character of the paper money in use in the United States may be attributed to the several causes of divided legislative and administrative authority and responsibility, the exigencies of party emergency and the partisanship of political caucuses,[1] and the complexity of the legislative organizations from which the enactments originating these paper issues have sprung. The fact that the creation and administration of the finances of the United States, which include all the money and currency in use,

---

[1] Upton, *Money in Politics*, p. 147.

are controlled by twenty-four committees
of the Congress [1] is ill calculated to arouse
the enthusiastic admiration of the man of
affairs; and especially must this be true,
when it is reflected that the men composing
these congressional committees are not
necessarily possessed of either special apti-
tude or special knowledge of the subject,
and are often prone to prefer party advantage to the public welfare in financial as in
other legislation.[2]

---

[1] Woodrow Wilson, *Congressional Government*, 10th ed., p.
136.

[2] *The Forum*, " Should the Government Retire from Banking?" Feb., 1895.

II.

THE Treasury Department of the government was established by the Congress, September 2, 1789. It had its germ in the scheme adopted in 1778 by the Continental Congress for the furtherance of the finances of the Revolution. This was what is known in history as the Board of Treasury, consisting at first of five delegates of the Congress, and later of fifteen, who had charge of the continental finances. A treasurer and auditor, and a comptroller were appointed ; and later commissioners of accounts. The scheme was inefficient and cumbersome as constituted ; and it was not until Robert Morris was made superintendent of the finances, and reorganized the Board of Treasury, that it became, even in a measure, adequate to deal with the perplexing questions of ways and means which

24

confronted the United Colonists. He resigned in 1784; and for the following five
years and until the establishment of the
Treasury Department on the plan of its
later organization, the finances of the government were in great confusion.[1]

When the House of Representatives
undertook to create a Treasury Department, the old Board of Treasury did not
lack its able and strenuous advocates, who
sought to perpetuate it, in spite of its un-
toward record; and, strange to say, though
indicative of the conflicting attitudes which
men's minds can assume at varying times
and under certain circumstances towards
questions of finance, as towards other governmental policies, among the adherents of
the old system there was none more conspicuously zealous in its behalf than Mr.
Elbridge Gerry, who had been formerly
one of its members, and one of its most
earnest condemners. But the efforts of its
friends failed, and the Board of Treasury
of the Continental Congress yielded to the
Treasury Department of the United States.

---

[1] *Lalor's Political Cyclopædia*, art., "American Finance."

It is an interesting fact that the old Board
of Treasury issued the first coins made by
authority of the government. They were
of copper, and known as "Fugios" from
the word " Fugio," which the statute of
the Congress enacted July 7, 1787, required
should appear on the face of the coin.[1]

The Constitution of the United States
makes no specific provision for a Federal
Treasury ; yet recognizes it by name in
article one, section nine. The Treasury
was established by act of the Congress
and from the time of its establishment up
to the organization of the Sub-Treasury,
was practically a legal entity without a
substantial existence.[2]

Under the numerous statutes enacted
since that creating the Treasury, the functions of this department of the government
have become very intricate, important, and
far-reaching in their results ;—perhaps more
so than of any other of the several executive departments.

The head of the Treasury Department is

[1] *Lalor's Cyclop.*, art., " Coinage."
[2] J. K. Upton, *Money in Politics*, ch. x.

the Secretary of the Treasury, who is one of the Cabinet officers, and by virtue of his office an adviser of the President of the United States on all matters appertaining to the finances. The law requires that he must be a person who is not in any way interested in trade or commerce.[1] His duties comprise, among many others not directly connected with the money and currency of the country, the preparation of schemes and plans for the public revenue and public credit, the making of annual and special reports with reference to the finances and to other matters of his department, and the performance of such additional fiscal offices as are required by law.

His reports are referred, when they reach the Congress, to the House Committee on Ways and Means, which is the great revenue-raising committee of the Congress. The annual reports of the Secretary of the Treasury are "in one respect the great yearly balance-sheets, exhibiting the receipts and expenditures of the government, its liabilities and its credits; and, in

[1] *Revised Statutes of U. S.,* § 243.

another aspect, general views of the state of industry and of the financial machinery of the country, summarizing the information compiled by the Bureau of Statistics with reference to the condition of the manufactures and of domestic trade, as well as with regard to the plight of the currency and of the national banks." [1]

The Secretary of the Treasury of the United States differs from the Finance Ministers of the great European powers in nothing more conspicuously than in the failure of legislation to provide that he shall be a member of the law-making body. Thus his official communications to the Congress, as has been stated, are required to be made in writing. In practice he is frequently summoned, or voluntarily appears, before the various committees of the Congress having to do with the finances, for the purpose of explaining some financial measure, or of advising some specific act of legislation; but such appearance is extra-official from a legislative standpoint.

---

[1] Woodrow Wilson, *Congressional Government*, 10th ed., p. 171.

" His function was of the utmost importance at the beginning of the government when a national system of finance had to be built up and the federal government rescued from its grave embarrassments. Hamilton, who then held the office, effected both. During the War of Secession, it again became powerful, owing to the enormous loans contracted and the quantities of paper money issued, and it remains so now, because it has the management (as far as Congress permits) of the currency and the national debt. The Secretary has, however, by no means the same range of action as a finance minister in European countries, for as he is excluded from Congress, although he regularly reports to it, he has nothing directly to do with the imposition of taxes, and very little with the appropriation of revenue to the various burdens of the state." [1]

Tho Secretary of the Treasury is not elected by the people, nor by the Congress; and is therefore responsible to neither. He is an appointee of the President; and while accountable to public opinion, cannot, as in England, be retired from office by a party vote, but is only subject to removal during the term of his appointment by impeachment. He may differ radically,

---

[1] James Bryce, *The American Commonwealth*, 2d ed., vol. i., p. 84.

and frequently does, from the Congress in his conception of public finance and currency measures; and his responsibility as a member of the Cabinet is individual and to the President alone.

After the organization of the Treasury Department and an outlining of the financial methods to be pursued by the government in its earlier history, the administration of the Treasury was by no means so beset with difficulties, dangers, and responsibilities as it has been since 1861. In the past thirty-five years its functions and operations have been wonderfully enlarged and extended under congressional currency and finance legislation. Without undertaking to state in detail the numerous and varied responsibilities and authorities of the Secretary in administering the affairs of the Treasury Department, mention should be made of three important powers conferred upon him by the Congress, viz.: of managing the Federal coinage and currency created and issued under congressional legislation, of controlling and supervising, through a subordinate officer of his department, the National Banking Associations, and of managing the public debt.

Of his many subordinates whose services are required for the necessary administration of the Department, it is only pertinent to the subject to mention those whose duties are directly in relation to the circulating medium of the country and the immediate currency transactions of the treasury itself.[1]

These subordinate officers are in the order of their relative importance as gauged by the Congress in fixing their several salaries by statute, as follows, viz.: The Treasurer of the United States, the Comptroller of the Currency, the two Assistant Secretaries of the Treasury, the Chief of the Bureau of Engraving and Printing, the Register of the Treasury, and the Director of the Mint. They are, like the Secretary himself, all appointed by the President, with the consent and advice of the Senate.

The Treasurer of the United States has

---

[1] An admirable sketch of the United States Treasury Department by Mr. A. R. Spofford may be found in *Lalor's Cyclopædia.*

charge of and is responsible for the public
moneys in the Treasury at Washington and
in the nine Sub-Treasuries located in the
most important cities of the country, as
well as of that deposited in those national
banks which are made United States depositories of public funds by statute. He
is trustee of the government bonds purchased and owned by national banks taking out circulation, and placed with him
for the purpose of securing the solvency of
the national bank notes; and among his
many other duties is that of agent of the
government for the redemption of these
notes of the banks. He has like charge of
the redemption of all other government
currency obligations.

The Comptroller of the Currency has
especial control, subject to the discretion
of the Secretary of the Treasury and to
the statutory limitations and restrictions
imposed by the Congress, of the national
banking system. He appoints bank examiners and receivers of broken banks;
and he collects and compiles statistics of
banks and banking, both State and Federal.

He has charge of the redemption and destruction of notes issued by the national banks which become so mutilated or otherwise injured as to be unfit for further use. It is his duty to make stated reports of his transactions to the Congress. He may not be interested in any national banking association; and no such association may be organized without his previous authority.

The statute creating the office of Comptroller of the Currency was enacted in 1863, and was a necessary part of the scheme of the national banking system suggested by Mr. Chase, Secretary of the Treasury in Mr. Lincoln's first administration.

The two Assistant Secretaries of the Treasury have a general subordinate control of the routine business of the department; and in the absence of the Secretary or in case of his inability to perform his duties, one of them is designated to act in his stead.

The Chief of the Bureau of Engraving and Printing has charge of that extensive section of the Department in which the

3

plates are prepared and the printing done therefrom of all government bonds, national bank notes, gold certificates, silver certificates and currency certificates, Treasury notes and internal revenue stamps. This Bureau grew out of the provisions of the second section of the act of July 11, 1862, directing the engraving and printing of the greenbacks, under the supervision of the Secretary of the Treasury, at the Department. It was reorganized and perfected in its details at a subsequent period by Secretary Sherman. A singular fact in connection with its history is that the policy of employing women in the public departments of government at Washington originated with this Bureau.[1]

The keeping of the government's fiscal accounts, and the signing and issuing of its bonds, notes, and certificates, are among the duties and responsibilities of the Register of the Treasury. In addition, he registers all warrants drawn by the Secretary of the Treasury upon the Treasurer of the United States ; and he is required to can-

---

[1] J. K. Upton, *Money in Politics*, pp. 92 and 93.

cel and destroy the Treasury notes which come into the Treasury in so mutilated or defaced a condition as to be unfit for further use.

Under the Coinage act of 1873, which, as will be seen hereafter, marks the beginning of an important epoch in the history of the currency of the United States, the Mint Bureau was made a special division of the Treasury Department. The Director of the Mint is the chief officer of the Mint Bureau; and is of course subordinate to the Secretary of the Treasury, and like the other Treasury officials, in certain directions, subject to his control. Prior to the passage of the Coinage act of 1873, the Director of the Mint at Philadelphia was the chief mint officer; and that mint was the principal one, of which the others were branches. Under the provisions of the act of 1873 each mint was made and remains independent of the others; and each is in charge of a superintendent who makes reports directly to the Director of the Mint at the Mint Bureau in Washington.[1] The

[1] *Lalor's Cyclopædia*, article "Coinage."

minor coinage is by law now confined to
the Philadelphia mint.[1]

The Director of the Mint formulates rules
and regulations for the government of the
mints and assay offices; and regulates the
distribution of the coinage of silver and the
charges to be collected of those who deposit it. The purchases of silver bullion
for the coinage of subsidiary silver and the
allotment of the coinage to the several
mints are under his immediate supervision;
and tests of the weight and fineness of coins
struck at the mints are made in the assay
laboratory at Washington under his charge.
He also estimates and fixes the values of the
standard coins of foreign countries for cus-
tom-house and other public purposes.

The fiscal year of the United States
Treasury in all matters of accounts, receipts, expenditures, estimates, and appro-
priations commences by law on the first day
of July in each year; and all accounts of
receipts and disbursements required by law
to be published annually are prepared and
published with reference thereto.[2]

---

[1] *Banker's Magazine* for April, 1895, p. 726.
[2] *United States Revised Statutes*, Title VII.

III.

It is not within the scope of these chapters to make more than brief and passing
reference to the financial events of the
earlier days of the Republic, when the
Federal government was engaged in the
banking business in connection with the
organization and maintenance of the first
and second Banks of the United States.
Few questions down to 1840 were so
prominent in national politics as that of a
National Bank ; and few currencies were
more satisfactory and popular in the financial history of any country than the notes
of the second Bank of the United States
for a period of twenty years of its existence.[1] When President Jackson removed

---

[1] *Lalor's Cyclopædia*, article " Bank Controversies."

the government deposits from the last-
named institution to the state banks, the
glory of the Federal Bank was at an end.[1]

The system adopted by Jackson, without
the express authority or sanction of law, of
depositing the government funds entirely
in banks chartered and governed exclusively
by state laws, was subsequently specifically
authorized by legislation of the Congress as
a part of the federal plan of finance; and
was followed within a few years by the
institution of what is known as the Sub-
Treasury or Independent Treasury system
of the United States.

Prior to the removal of the deposits by
Jackson, in addition to the United States
Bank the government under special contracts made use of certain state banks as
depositories of public moneys; but always
with the proviso that the state bank should
on request transfer to the Bank of the
United States any money received in excess
of the permanent deposit; and a number of
state banks were so used by the Secretary
of the Treasury up to the time of the re-

---

[1] *Lalor's Cyclopædia*, article " Independent Treasury."

moval of the deposits. By the act creating the Bank, the Secretary was directed to deposit all public moneys in the Bank or its branches, " unless the Secretary of the Treasury shall at any time otherwise order and direct; in which case the Secretary of the Treasury shall immediately lay before Congress, if in session, and if not, immediately after the commencement of the next session, the reason of such order or direction."

The President believed that the Bank of the United States under the management of Nicholas Biddle, was not only not safely managing the government's finances, but was endeavoring, through discounts and loans to members of the Congress and powerful politicians, to so control the Congress as to secure the impeachment of himself and other prominent members of his administration. Under the instructions of the Executive, who assumed full responsibility therefor, Roger B. Taney, subsequently Chief Justice of the United States, and who three days before had been appointed Secretary of the Treasury for the purpose by Jackson, gave the necessary orders for the removal. As a matter of fact, however, there was no removal. The government funds on deposit with the Bank were left there. The order of the Secretary provided that the public moneys should thereafter be deposited in certain state banks, specifically set out therein. In speaking of the Bank's controversy with Jackson, Professor Alexander Johnston says:

"Instead of following the simple and natural plan afterwards adopted of an Independent Treasury, by which the whole fiscal business of the Federal government was intrusted to the Treasury, Congress had undertaken to graft a private corporation upon the Treasury. The larger the fiscal business of the country grew, the more powerful and dangerous grew this extra-governmental excrescence. The very even balance of the war between the President and the Bank is of itself strong evidence of the power which the Bank was able to exert in politics so early in our history as 1831–32. Had it continued to enjoy the use of the increasing revenues of the Federal government, it would have become more and more dangerous, either as the tool or as the master of a popular government, and the succeeding administrations would have found it more and more difficult to shake off its weight." [1]

---

[1] *Lalor's Cyclopædia*, article "Removal of Deposits."

As far back as 1834, William F. Gordon, a member of Congress from Albemarle County, Virginia, and a disciple and personal friend of Thomas Jefferson, devised the scheme of the Independent Treasury, and introduced in the Congress a bill providing for its establishment.[1] The measure was dropped| at that time| for lack of the support which it subsequently obtained when made a party measure by a vigorous and determined Executive, receiving on its first introduction in the Congress only thirty-three votes. President Van Buren, soon after his inauguration, found his administration beset by financial difficulties, and the government at a loss for money to defray its current expenses. In a message to the extra-session of the Congress which convened September 4, 1837, he advocated the separation of the fiscal matters of government from all banking business and banking corporations, suggesting and adopting as a party measure Gordon's Sub-Treasury scheme.[2] This scheme was, in

[1] David Kinley, *The Independent Treasury of the United States*, p. 25.

[2] *The Statesman's Manual*, 2d ed., vol. ii., p. 1051.

effect that the government revenues, instead
of being deposited in certain favored banks,
called in the political slang of the day,
"pet banks," as had been done since the
removal of the deposits, "should be left in
the hands of assistant cashiers or treasurers
at convenient and permanent points throughout the country, to be disbursed or accounted for to the Secretary of the Treasury by
such assistant treasurers, who were required
to give bond for the faithful performance
of their duties."

Silas Wright, of New York, on January
16, 1838, reported the Independent Treasury bill from the Senate Committee on
Finance. It passed the Senate, and was
defeated in the House of Representatives.
Mr. Calhoun had been in favor of the bill
originated in 1834 by Gordon; but voted
against the Wright bill because that portion of the original plan providing for a
" hard money " currency was stricken out.[1]
In January, 1840, Mr. Wright again introduced his bill in the Senate, where it was

---

[1] W. Cluskey, *Political Text Book*, article " Independent
Treasury."

passed. On June 30, 1840, it passed the House of Representatives, and became a law. In June, 1841, Mr. Clay from the Senate Finance Committee, introduced a bill to repeal the Independent Treasury law enacted the year before. The repeal bill passed both Houses of the Congress, and was signed by President Tyler. The Congress of 1841 was a Whig Congress, and in favor of re-establishing a National Bank. A bill for that purpose was passed by the Congress, but was vetoed by the President on constitutional grounds.[1]

The Independent Treasury act, now on the Federal statute book, became a law on August 6, 1846 ;[2] and though amended in many minor details by direct enactment, and diverted from its original purposes by sundry acts of congressional currency legislation, stands in general form as it was originally framed by its author.

There are nine sub-treasuries at the present time, located respectively at Balti-

---

[1] Cluskey, *Political Text Book*, article " Independent Treasury."

[2] Kinley, *The Independent Treasury*, p. 271.

more, Philadelphia, New York, Boston, Cincinnati, Chicago, St. Louis, New Orleans, and San Francisco. Of these the most important, on account of its location and of the magnitude of its transactions, is that in the city of New York. By the provisions of the act passed in 1875 for the resumption of specie payments, the suspension of which by the sub-treasuries took place December 28, 1861,[1] the legal tender United States note known as the greenback was made redeemable only at the sub-treasury in the city of New York.[2] By subsequent legislation the sub-treasury at San Francisco was also authorized to redeem the greenback in "specie";[3] and these two sub-treasuries remain the only ones at which such redemption may be made.

Although the Independent Treasury plan as formulated and adopted,[4] contem-

---

[1] *Lalor's Cyclopædia*, article " American Finance."

[2] Act, January 14, 1875.

[3] Act, March 3, 1887. *Supplement to Revised Statutes*, p. 566.

[4] " The primary purpose of the adoption of the Independent Treasury was the safety of the public money."—Kinley, *The Independent Treasury*, p. 220.

plated primarily nothing further than a better organization of the Treasury in its methods of business, and the proper collection, safe-keeping, and disbursement of the public revenues; or, as stated by Mr. Calhoun in his speech on the Independent Treasury bill, delivered in the Senate, February 15, 1838, "to take the public money out of the hands of the Executive and place it under the control of the laws, and to prevent the renewal of a connection which has proved so unfortunate to the government and the banks,"[1] Federal legislation subsequent to 1860, without materially altering the tenor and form of the Sub-Treasury act, has given to the general Treasury system an incomparably greater latitude and significance than it possessed in its earlier history, and has incorporated into its operation features, which, if not at variance with those original provisions of the law, were at least never anticipated in the purview of its first plan.[2] It is difficult

---

[1] Calhoun's *Works*, vol. iii., p. 203.

[2] Kinley, *The Independent Treasury of the United States*, p. 122.

to imagine, for example, in the light of the politico-economic controversies over a National Bank, which the final definite establishment of the Sub-Treasury in a measure settled and disposed of, that section eighteen of the act of August 6, 1846, which provided that "all duties, taxes, sales of public lands, debts, and sums of money accruing or becoming due to the United States, and also all sums due for postages, or otherwise to the General Post-office Department, shall be paid in gold and silver coin only, or in Treasury notes issued under the authority of the United States," would ultimately be used for the conversion of the Independent Treasury of the United States into a National Bank of issue, with an irredeemable circulation of $500,000,000 of legal tender paper notes, and the necessary concomitant of a one hundred million dollar gold reserve.[1]

The financial war-policy, which conceived and created the greenback, with a legal tender feature approved by the judicial

---

[1] "The Financial Muddle," by Henry G. Cannon, in the *North American Review* for February, 1895.

determination of the highest Federal tribunal; the compulsory enactment of the
Congress which makes the greenback redeemable in coin on presentation, and requires it to be re-issued immediately on
redemption by the Treasury Department;
and the further financial legislation by the
Congress, authorizing not only the accumulation of silver bullion in the Treasury and
the coinage of silver dollars on a false ratio,
but the issue of certificates of deposit and
Treasury promises to pay against such dollars and bullion, and defining the policy of
the government to be the practical payment
of the greenbacks, silver certificates and
Treasury notes in gold coin, have combined
to create new functions, duties, and purposes, and to set into motion other systems
of financial machinery than those known to
the earlier administration of the Treasury
Department.[1] Before the enactment of this
later legislation " the Sub-Treasury system
as originally established so entirely severed
the government from the money market
that, fortunately, the bankers and mer-

[1] Calhoun's *Works*, vol. iii., p. 231.

chants could afford to laugh at the insignificance of the government on their arena;
but its position was never so strong or sound
as when, in this point of view, it was most
ridiculous."[1] Under the latter day enlarge-
ment of the Treasury functions by the Congress, when the government is put to the
gravest exertions to keep its paper issues
at par by the maintenance of a gold reserve
in the Treasury, and when the national
banks, by a judicious use of government
legal tenders, control the gold reserve and
the government's bond issues availed of to
maintain it, the relations existing between
the government and the money market have
become of such a peculiar character that the
Treasury's insignificance in any struggle
between the two becomes again ridiculous
from another standpoint than the one just
named.

In the view of those who hold that there
should be an entire separation of the government from banks and banking, the idea
that the Congress itself can create money
by its simple *fiat* or sanction, has, under the

---

[1] W. G. Sumner, *History of American Currency*, p. 167.

influence of the legislation above described, taken strong hold upon the public mind. They assert, too, that while the Federal Treasury is now compelled by statute to perform the offices of a bank of issue, [1] its executive officer is hampered with requirements and limitations, frequently enacted by the Congress for special purposes or to meet impending emergencies, which either retard or absolutely prevent his efforts to conduct the business of his great national bank with any degree of discretion or expectation of success. [2]

To the contrary, however, are the opinions of those of an opposing school, who in advocating the propriety of the enlarged uses of the Sub-Treasury system, assert that the government's recent failures to maintain the gold reserve in the Treasury, and the resultant necessity for the sale of bonds to protect it, have sprung from congressional legislation affecting the raising of public revenues, and not from currency conditions;

---

[1] " The Financial Muddle," *North Am. Review* for February, 1895.

[2] *Report of the Secretary of the Treasury*, December, 1894.

and contend that "under the existing system, by which the government practically
holds and disburses its own money and that
of its officers, the fiscal operations are conducted without disturbance, embarrass-
ment, or favoritism, and with satisfaction
to all concerned."[1]

While the assertion of Professor Kinley,
in his elaborate and able treatise on the
Independent Treasury, that the Sub-Treasury act made the government distinctively
its own banker, and taken in connection
with the law sanctioning the emission of
treasury notes, established a bank of issue,
is true in degree and in theory, the provision of the law authorizing treasury notes
and of that section of the Sub-Treasury act
permitting their acceptance at the sub-
treasuries for sums due the government,
were secondary considerations in the establishment of the Independent Treasury. At
no time in the history of the country after
the passage of the Sub-Treasury act, prior
to the legal tender legislation of 1862, had

---

[1] Secretary John Sherman, in 1880; cited in Kinley's *The Independent Treasury*, p. 77.

the business of issuing notes been in vogue
with the Treasury, save to a very limited
and exceptional extent; and at no time
prior to that period had the government
ever found it necessary to maintain in its
vaults a large and unimpaired gold reserve
to secure the redemption of such treasury
notes as were issued. But when, as Mr.
Kinley subsequently says,[1] the government
"turned itself to the manufacture by the
hundred million of greenbacks, which by a
legal tender *fiat* were forced on creditors in
payment of the hard-earned dollars they
had loaned, from this time on, certainly,
until the resumption of specie payments,
the Sub-Treasury law was a dead letter,"
and the Sub-Treasury itself remained "only
in form." The subsequent passage of the
National Bank act, which made the national
bank notes issued thereunder receivable at
their nominal value everywhere in the
United States in all payments to and by
the government, except customs and interest
on the public debt, was a practical nullifi-
cation of the provision of the Sub-Treasury

[1] p. 68.

act, which limited payments to and by the government to gold and silver and treasury notes. A further departure from the intent and purpose of the original law was the issuing under act of the Congress, of gold and silver certificates, which are in effect certificates of the government that so much gold and silver coin respectively has been deposited in the sub-treasuries, and is held free of charge for the convenience of the holders of such certificates.

In 1872 the Congress went still further in departing from the old Sub-Treasury land-marks when it passed the act providing that the banks might deposit legal tender notes in the sub-treasuries and receive certificates of deposit known as "currency certificates," of large denominations, prepared and issued by the Treasury without cost to the banks.[1] The legal tenders so deposited are withdrawable on demand, and by this arrangement the banks are always in position to be supplied with legal tender notes of small and convenient denominations, without expense.[2]

---

[1] Act, June 8, 1872.
[2] Kinley, *The Independent Treasury*, p. 72.

In the progress of legislative events since 1860, the transactions of the Sub-Treasury have become necessarily so intermingled with the business of the banks as that the two systems are absolutely interdependent. A people who had been taught to believe that the agencies of national banks in a Republican form of government were undesirable, now submits with apparent indifference to the existence of a double system of national banks, the one carried on directly by the government in its administration of the Treasury, and the other sanctioned and created by the government but carried on by private individuals, who are in the habit of taking the government by the throat whenever they are pleased to do so.

"The divorce of the government and the banks" has ceased to be; and the Sub-Treasury system, instead of existing "in form only," has become under congressional legislation a gigantic national banking scheme, dominated by party politics, in comparison with which the first and second Banks of the United States were insignificant. What the Sub-Treasury in its earlier form and purpose accomplished for the government, as told in the language of a learned, impartial, and conservative author-ity, may not inappropriately conclude this chapter :

"It inflicted no damage upon the state banks or upon business at large ; it did not increase the num-ber of offices at the disposal of the president and his party, or the power of the president over the commercial interests of the country ; it laid no 'corner stone of despotism' ; its practical operation was much more smooth and successful than might have been anticipated in a civil service already so far debased ; and it plainly relieved the govern-ment from any except indirect and remote conse-quences of suspension of specie payments by the banks, and the country from the difficulties and dangers incident to the control of a national bank by a representative body. Its passage opened a hitherto unthought of door of escape from a na-tional bank, so inviting that it would have been foolish for the dominant party not to have availed itself of it, and so convenient when tried, that it would have been impossible on a fair test to induce the country to retrace its steps. Only the momen-tum of the Whig party proper, acquired by years of struggle for a national bank, compelled its leaders to keep up for a time a contest whose futility they were quick to perceive. The first successful execu-tion of the independent treasury act made a national bank an impossibility with general popular consent, and completed the 'divorce of bank and state' for which the president had for three years been exerting all his energy and influence." [1]

---

[1] Prof. Alexander Johnston in *Lalor's Cyclopædia*, article " Independent Treasury."

IV.

THE method of organizing a national bank, and its powers and functions when organized, are specifically provided by enactment of the Congress, known as the National Bank Act. The minimum capital stock of a national bank in places of less than six thousand population must be $50,-000; in places between six thousand and fifty thousand population $100,000; and in cities of fifty thousand population or more $200,000.[1] After the requisite amount of stock has been subscribed, one half of it must be paid up before the bank can begin business; and the residue is payable in instalments in the five succeeding months.[2]

The functions and powers of the national

---

[1] *Rev. Statutes, U. S.*, § 5138.
[2] *Rev. Statutes, U. S.*, § 5140.

banks are to receive deposits, to discount
and negotiate commercial paper, to buy and
sell exchange, coin, and bullion ; to lend
money on personal security, and to issue
and circulate bank notes as currency.[1] Restrictions of various kinds are imposed
upon the banks, with a view of compelling
the safe and proper conduct of their business, such as inhibitions against engaging
in general trade and commerce, against
holding real estate except in certain specified instances, and the like. A further and
salutary provision is that there shall be a
ratable liability on the stockholder for the
debts of the bank to the extent of his
stockholding, in addition to the capital
actually invested by him.

The charters of the national banks, which
are issued from the Treasury Department
on application of not less than five corporators to the Comptroller of the Currency,
are in the nature of certificates from that
officer that the preliminary requirements
of the statute have been complied with.
The organization certificate, preliminary to

[1] *Rev. Statutes, U. S.,* § 5136.

the issuing by the Comptroller of the certificate of incorporation, must contain the
name of the association ; the name of the
place where its operations of discount and
deposit are to be carried on; the amount
of capital stock, and the number of shares
into which the same is to be divided; the
names and places of residence of the share-
holders, and the number of shares held by
each; and the fact that the certificate is
made to enable the corporators to avail
themselves of the advantages of the National Bank act.[1]

In addition to the powers and functions
described, such of the national banks as are
so designated may become depositories of
certain of the public moneys, and are required to place with the Treasurer of the
United States at Washington government
bonds as security for the safe-keeping and
proper handling of such funds.[2]   This provision is in the nature of a return by the
government to the practice prevailing after
the removal of the deposits from the second

---

[1] *Rev. Statutes U. S.,* § 5134.
[2] *Rev. Statutes U. S.,* § 5153.

National Bank of the United States by
President Jackson, prior to the passage of
the Independent Treasury act, described
in the preceding chapter.[1]

The currency in the shape of bank notes
is printed at the Treasury Department in
Washington, from plates prepared by the
Bureau of Engraving and Printing from
designs authorized by the Secretary of the
Treasury, upon " distinctive " paper, the
material used in the manufacture of which
is a government secret. The possession by
any person of this " distinctive " paper,
other than those authorized by law, is made
a felony, punishable by fine and imprisonment at hard labor.[2]

Under the act of 1864, the notes issued
by the Treasury Department might amount
by law to ninety per cent. of the market
value of the bonds deposited to secure
them, but could not exceed ninety per cent.
of the par value of such bonds if bearing
interest at a rate not less than five per
cent.; and in no case might exceed the

---

[1] *Lalor's Cyclopædia*, article, " Bank Controversies."
[2] *Rev. Statutes U. S.*, § 5430.

capital stock of the banks. This provision
was modified the following year so that
banks with a capital of from $50,000 to
$500,000 might receive in circulating notes
only ninety per cent. of their capital, and
so on in a diminishing percentage as the
capital of the bank increases.[1]

Under the existing provision of the National Bank act, notes may be issued to
the bank by the Treasury Department to
the extent of ninety per cent. of the par
value of the bonds so deposited.[2] Thus,
for example, before a national bank can
take out $9,000 of circulating notes, it
must deposit interest-bearing government
bonds of the par value of $10,000. These
bonds command a premium in the market,
so that $10,000 of government four per
cents. would cost the bank $11,550. The
law requires the deposit with the United
States Treasurer at Washington of five per
cent. of its circulation in money by each
national bank for a redemption fund. So
the bank can only issue $9,000 of notes
after the expenditure of $12,000 in money.[3]

[1] H. W. Richardson, *The National Banks*, chap. v.
[2] Act, July 12, 1882, § 10.
[3] W. L. Trenholm, *The People's Money*, p. 169.

The five per cent. redemption fund is required by the statute to be deposited in "lawful money of the United States."[1] This may be counted as a part of the bank's legal reserve. It is further provided in the same section of the statute, that when the bank's circulating notes shall be presented for redemption in sums of one thousand dollars, or any multiple thereof, to the Treasurer of the United States, the same shall be redeemed in United States notes.

When the bank notes have once gone out and mingle with the general circulating medium they are never brought back to the bank which issues them for redemption, differing in this respect from the real bank note in its genuine sense, which is redeemed by the bank that issues it, and when so redeemed is never reissued. At no time, however, can the national bank withdraw its bonds on deposit for the security of the outstanding notes until it has made a deposit of lawful money for their redemption.

It is seen at once that the national bank note is a promise of the United States gov-

---

[1] Act, June 20, 1874, § 3.

ernment to pay, based upon the security of government bonds, bought by the bank issuing the notes, and deposited as a pledge with the Treasurer at Washington.

The law provides for the immediate redemption at the Treasury of all the notes of any failed bank.[1] The destruction of any bank notes in circulation is a loss to the bank issuing them and enures to the gain of the government, as does also the failure of ultimate holders of the notes to call for their redemption at the Treasury.[2]

Frequent reports, not less than five in number, of the condition of the banks are required by the Comptroller of the Currency each year. These itemized reports, made out on printed forms setting forth the sundry items required to be stated, are published in the local papers of the town or city where the bank making them is conducted;[3] and each bank is subject at any time to the visitation and inspection of special Treasury agents, appointed by the Comptroller of the Currency, known as

---

[1] *Rev. Statutes U. S.*, § 5224.
[2] Act, July 12, 1882, § 6.
[3] *Rev. Statutes U. S.*, § 5211.

bank examiners, who report to him the condition of each bank examined by them.[1]
The expenses of publishing the reports
made by the banks, and of the investiga-
tions conducted by the bank examiners,
are borne by the individual bank in each
instance.

A tax of one per cent. per annum is imposed upon the banks' circulation by the
government, and of one half of one per cent.
upon their average deposits and capital not
invested in United States bonds.[2] Up to
the passage by the Congress on August 13,
1894, of the act to subject to state taxation
national bank notes and United States
Treasury notes, such notes were exempt
from local taxation of any kind. They are
by that act now made subject to taxation
as money on hand or on deposit under the
laws of any state or territory, provided
that such taxation is exercised in the same
manner and at the same rate that such
state or territory taxes money, or currency
circulating as money, within its jurisdiction.

The act of March 3, 1887, provides that

[1] *Rev. Statutes U. S.*, § 5240.
[2] *Rev. Statutes U. S.*, § 5214.

for the protection of depositors from liability, the banks outside of the "reserve cities" shall keep a reserve of 15 per cent. of their deposits, and that banks in the "reserve cities" shall keep 25 per cent. Any city having fifty thousand inhabitants can become a "reserve city" upon application of three fourths of the national banks established and doing business in it; and a city having two hundred thousand inhabitants can be made a "central reserve city" upon application of three fourths of the national banks established in it.[1] This statute further provides that one half of the lawful money reserve of the national banks located in other reserve cities may be deposited in such central reserve cities.

The report of the Comptroller of the Currency made to the Congress, December 3, 1894, shows that on October 2, 1894, there were 3755 national banks in existence in the United States having an outstanding bank note circulation of $172,331,978. On October 3, 1893, there were 3781 national banks having an outstanding note circula-

---

[1] C. F. Dunbar, *The Theory and History of Banking*, p. 145 ; *Supplement to the Revised Code*, vol. i., p. 566.

tion of $182,959,725. The total amount
of outstanding bank circulation, including
not only the notes of the banks still in
operation, but of the large number that suspended during the panic of 1893 and which
had not as yet been redeemed, aggregated
October 31, 1894 the sum of $207,472,603.[1]

Under the original bank act, the life of a
national bank was limited to twenty years.[2]
In 1882 the Congress enacted what is
known as "the bank charter extension
act,"[3] providing that upon compliance with
certain requirements therein specified, the
bank might further extend its corporate
existence, with the approval of the Comptroller of the Currency, for another twenty
years. This amendment of the National
Bank act, though of extreme importance
in prolonging the existence of the associations, made little change in the general provisions of the law governing the national
banks. The ultimate payment at a probably comparatively early date of the national
debt, on which the circulation of the na-

---

[1] *Report of the Secretary of the Treasury*, 1894, p. **xv.**
[2] *Rev. Statutes U. S.*, § 5136.
[3] Act, July 12, 1882.

tional banks is based, makes it inevitable that the national bank system must then come to an end, so far as the issuing of notes is concerned, unless some acceptable modification or change shall be made in the law, which will either provide a different character of pledged security, or make the notes so issued "bank notes" in the true sense of the term—that is, an issue based on the general assets and credit of the bank, with proper provision for their prompt redemption.

The bankers and financiers of the country, recognizing the necessity of anticipating the payment of the government's debt, have for some years past been engaged in considering plans and schemes for a proper bank currency; and the advocates of state banks of issue, subject to such legal control and restriction as will secure the solvency of their notes, are to be found among the most distinguished and well informed men of affairs and publicists in America.

The fact, however, that the people of the United States have for so long a period known no other bank note than that issued by the national banks, which, despite other objections urged against it, has steadily maintained the inherent qualities of absolute safety and ready receivability everywhere throughout the Republic makes the progress of those currency reformers who advocate state banks of issue a difficult one. To this public sentiment in favor of the national bank note and against state bank circulation may be added the more insuperable one of a clearly indicated determination on the part of the Congress to relax nothing of its iron grasp upon the entire currency of the country. Repeated efforts have been made in successive sessions of the Congress to secure the repeal of the ten per cent. tax on state bank issues, only to be met in each case with signal defeat. The most conspicuous instance of this deep-seated determination in the Congress has been the rejection, at a late session, of this measure of repeal by a House of Representatives elected on a party platform which in express terms declared in favor of the repeal of this tax.[1]

---

[1] National Democratic Platform of 1892. *World Almanac* for 1893, p. 80.

V.

THE Clearing-Houses of the United States, though constituting one of the most conspicuous and important features of modern banking in connection with the currency circulation, form no part of the statutory machinery of the national government for the administration of its financial and money affairs. They exist under no provision of congressional enactment; though they are recognized by the government to the extent that the Sub-Treasury in the city of New York is a member of the clearing-house association of that city, having been admitted as such in 1879.[1] The system of clearing bank balances through the medium of such associations in the larger cities is one that was originated and perfected and is now carried on entirely for the conven-

---

[1] Kinley, *The Independent Treasury*, p. 77.

ience of the several banks adopting it. The Congress, however, has given practical recognition of the existence of these organizations, created under the influence of those unerring laws of business which even the most stringent legislation cannot always repress or divert, in two of its very notable statutes with regard to the currency. Under the act of June, 1872, a certain species of circulating medium, limited in its circulating quality by reason of its peculiar purposes, but none the less currency, known as " currency certificates," was created for the convenience of the clearing-houses. In a later act[1] the Congress provided that national banks should not be members of such clearing-house associations as refused to receive the government's gold and silver certificates in settlement of balances. Both of these provisions of the statute law have failed of the purpose for which they were intended, as will be hereafter shown : the former in that the currency certificates have been availed of by the banks for the accomplishment of purposes not anticipated when

---

[1] Act, July 12, 1882.

they were authorized by law; and the latter, in that the banks pay little if any attention to the provision, and continue members of such associations as do in point of fact refuse and decline to accept the silver certificate in settling balances.[1]

The operations of the clearing-houses which are purely voluntary associations of the banks doing business in individual localities, though governed by rigid and vigorously enforced rules and regulations of their own making, have received local legislative recognition in various ways and instances, notably in the provision of certain state statutes that presentment and demand through the clearing-house shall be as lawful as if at the bank itself.[2]

"Clearing" is defined as "the settlement of mutual claims by the payment of differences."[3] The advantages flowing from the operations of the New York Clearing-House Association, which is the largest and most important association of the kind in the

---

[1] Upton, *Money in Politics*, p. 225.

[2] Albert S. Bolles, *Practical Banking*, 7th ed., p. 236.

[3] *Lalor's Cyclopædia*, article "Clearing Houses."

United States, have been stated among others, by an eminent authority, as follows, viz.: First, the condensation for each bank belonging to the association of all the balances of all the banks connected therewith into one, and the settlement of that balance with little loss of time or trouble; second, the avoidance by the individual bank of numerous accounts, entries, and postings; third, great saving of time to the bank messengers, and a no less saving of risk in making exchanges and settlements from bank to bank; fourth, relief from a tremendous amount of labor and annoyance to which the cashiers, tellers, and book-keepers were subjected under the old system; fifth, the liberation of the associated banks from all injurious interdependence on each other; and finally, the absolute facility afforded by the books of the clearing-house association for knowing at all times the management and standing of every bank in the association.[1]

While the several clearing-houses in the

---

[1] Geo. D. Lyman, as quoted in Bolles' *Practical Banking*, p. 247.

United States differ in their organization
and processes in minor details, their purposes and methods are essentially the same
in all cities where they exist. At a fixed
hour in the morning of each day, a clerk
and a messenger or porter is sent from
every bank belonging to the association to
the Clearing-House. The clerks, at a given
signal from the manager of the Clearing-
House, are all seated at the desks provided
for them; and the messenger of each bank
in turn at another signal, delivers to each
of the clerks of the other banks the checks
or "exchanges" which his bank holds
against them. These checks or exchanges
have been made up into packages at the
bank sending them to the Clearing-House
prior to the daily session of the association;
and attached to each package is a statement
in figures of the amount of "exchanges"
contained therein. The paper thus "exchanged" or "cleared" consists of checks,
drafts, and certified notes. Bank notes
may be, but as a matter of practice are not
now so included, because the notes of the
national banks are treated not as "ex-

change" subject to presentation and payment, but as money. Formerly they were included in the Clearing-House "exchanges," especially in the time of the circulation of the state bank issues.

The messengers take receipts as they deliver these packages. When all the packages have been delivered, each bank in the association has before its clerk or representative all the checks or "exchanges" held against it by the other banks and has presented to all the other banks all the checks or "exchanges" it holds against them. Balances are then struck by the clerks as they sit at their desks in the Clearing-House, fines being imposed by the presiding officer for mistakes or delays; and a tally sheet of all the transactions is thereupon made by the manager of the association, on which tally-sheet the debits and credits of all the several banks must necessarily balance. The debit balances are required by the rules to be settled within a specified time, under penalties which are rigidly enforced.

This process of "clearing" takes but a

few minutes in each day, and is the only successful method ever devised for the prompt and accurate settlement and adjustment of exchanges among a number of banks. Errors subsequently ascertained, as when, for example, checks are thrown out, are corrected and settled between bank and bank, and not with the clearing-house, whose functions are at an end when the balances have been struck on the association tally sheet and the debit balances paid.[1] Debit balances, as ascertained by the tally sheet, are settled with coin or legal tender paper, as a rule. One of the most frequent means of settlement at the New York Clearing-House in the earlier days of its existence was by certificates of the Clearing-House itself, secured on gold deposited by the bank taking out the certificates. Other means of settling balances are with United States gold certificates, and with United States currency certificates, which last is a species of the currency

---

[1] R. G. Horr in *N. Y. Semi-Weekly Tribune,* July 21, 1893. Bolles' *Practical Banking,* Part III., p. 215 *et seq. Lalor's Cyclopædia,* article " Clearing Houses."

ostensibly provided by the Congress for
the express use of the banks in settling
such balances.[1] As heretofore stated, the
Congress has sought to compel by statute
the acceptance of the silver certificates by
the clearing-houses in settlement of balances, but in practice the law is not complied with, even at the New York Clearing-
House, of which the Sub-Treasury in that
city is a member.[2]

The clearing-house gold certificates
originated in 1853. They are issued, as
stated, against gold coin deposited to secure
them, and are in denominations of \$1,000,
\$5,000, and \$10,000. They are numbered,
registered, and endorsed by the bank issuing them; and are only used in settlements
between the banks. When in 1862 the
United States Government began its legal
tender issues, and gold and silver disappeared from circulation on the suspension
of specie payments, the clearing-house gold

---

[1] Act, June 8, 1872. *Compilation U. S. Currency Laws,*
p. 30.

[2] Act, July 12, 1882. J. K. Upton, *Money in Politics,*
p. 225.

certificates, of course, went out of use. In 1879, however, with the resumption of specie payments as the result of the Resumption act of 1875, they again reappeared.[1]

The United States gold certificates above referred to as in use for the settlement of clearing-house balances, are those first issued under act of March 3, 1863, and later under act of July 12, 1882, which are in circulation as a part of the general currency medium of the country. They are more specifically described in a subsequent chapter.[2] The use of United States gold certificates and currency certificates has in large measure superseded that of clearing house gold certificates in the settlement of bank balances at the clearing-houses.

The currency certificates were first issued by the Secretary of the Treasury under act of June 18, 1872, and are in denominations of not less than $5,000.[3] While they are not properly Treasury notes, but are

---

[1] Bolles' *Practical Banking*, p. 239.

[2] Post, chapter x.

[3] *Rev. Statutes U. S.*, § 5193.

certificates that legal tenders to the amount stated on the face of each have been deposited with the Treasury, they are permitted by law to be counted by the national banks as part of their legal reserve, and are included in the currency statements of the Treasury Department.[1] They are more fully described hereafter in the chapter treating of government certificates and Treasury notes.

The first clearing-house established in the United States was that of New York in 1853. Since its foundation it has been the most important one, the city of its location bearing to the country at large the financial relation which London bears to Great Britain.[2] The importance of the New York Clearing-House has been increased since the United States Sub-Treasury became a member of it in 1879.

Albert Gallatin, the great Federal financier, had proposed in 1841 the establishment of a clearing-house in New York City, having in mind the successful and

---

[1] *Report of the Secretary of the Treasury*, 1894.
[2] Walter Bagehot, *Lombard Street*, chapter ii.

beneficial operations of similar organizations theretofore in existence in London and Edinburgh. But the credit for the establishment and subsequent development of the association at New York is due in large measure to Mr. Geo. D. Lyman, who was its first manager, and continued for many years to conduct its operations in the most skilful and successful manner.[1] Since the establishment of the New York Clearing-House, others have been started in rapid succession in the larger cities, until at the present time there are in the United States more than eighty cities in which bank balances are adjusted through the medium of clearing-house associations.[2]

Since 1853, when it was organized, it has happened that on five occasions in time of great financial stringency and depression, the New York Clearing-House has resorted to the use of "loan certificates," generally known as "clearing-house certificates."[3]

---

[1] Bolles' *Practical Banking,* p 247.
[2] R. G. Horr in *N. Y. Semi-Weekly Tribune,* July 21, 1893.
[3] Dunbar, *Theory and History of Banking,* ch. vi., p. 67 *et seq.*

The bank desiring to obtain such certificates deposits with the officers of the clearing-house its promissory note for the amount desired, and puts up collateral securities aggregating in value twenty-five per cent. more than the amount of the loan sought. These securities are subjected to the scrutiny and must meet the approval of the loan committee of the clearing-house. When the deposits have been made and approved, the loan certificates, which are evidences of the united credit of all the banks belonging to the association, are issued by the clearing-house, in sums of $5,000 and multiples thereof, to the banks for the settlement of balances. The banks using them must pay six per cent. interest on their notes given for the loan of the certificates, which interest is distributable among all the banks of the association. The collateral securities on which the loan is made by the clearing-house must be kept good while the loan certificate is outstanding; and where any of the securities mature they are substituted by others. It follows as a natural consequence that when

money becomes worth less than six per cent.,
the loan certificates are retired.[1] By this arrangement the banks belonging to the association were enabled to expand their loans,
the special reserves held by them being
treated as a common fund, and when necessary, equalized among the banks by assess-
ments laid upon the stronger for the benefit
of the weaker. The practical effect of this
arrangement was that whenever a bank
needed an unusual amount of specie, it had
the backing of the combined reserves of all
the clearing-house banks.[2]

The five several occasions above referred
to in the history of the country, when the
banks of New York have been compelled
to resort to the combination of their reserves and the issue of clearing-house loan
certificates, have been respectively, November 1860, September 1873, May 1884, November 1890,[3] and August 1893.[4]

Similar certificates were resorted to by

[1] R. G. Horr in *N. Y. Tribune*, July 21, 1893.
[2] Dunbar, *Theory and History of Banking*, pp. 70, 71.
[3] Dunbar, *Theory and History of Banking*, ch. vi.
[4] W. D. Dabney, *Paper Money: Va. State Bar Asso'n Report*, 1894.

many of the clearing-house associations of other cities during the panic of 1893; and the stringency of the money market through their effective instrumentality was successfully diminished to the extent of their issues.

A question was raised in 1893 as to the liability of the banks thus using these clearing-house loan certificates to the payment of the ten per cent. tax imposed upon certain circulating notes by the act of March 3, 1865. The question was submitted by the Secretary of the Treasury to the Attorney-General, who decided that they were not subject to the tax in question.[1]

The Federal Sub-Treasury at New York became a member of the Clearing-House Association of that city in 1879, as a part of the scheme of the resumption of specie payments by the government under provisions of the Resumption act which went into effect in January of that year.

"Under this arrangement," says Mr. J. K. Upton, late Assistant Secretary of the Trea-

---

[1] W. D. Dabney, *Paper Money : Va. State Bar Asso'n Report*, 1894.

6

ury, "in consideration of the government's receiving and collecting the checks through the clearing-house, that body agreed to receive all balances due it upon such checks at the counter of the Sub-Treasury in that city, and to accept legal tender notes in payment of government checks and drafts of all descriptions. As all interest checks, as well as checks issued in payment of called bonds, were by law payable in coin, this agreement on the part of the clearing-house, through which institution nearly all of the checks passed, relieved the Treasury almost entirely from the necessity of making actual coin payments after resumption took place. This necessity being removed, there was no longer any reason for requiring duties and imports to be paid in coin, as provided by law;"[1] and as the result of the government's connection with the money market through the association of the Sub-Treasury with the clearing-house, coin ceased to be paid at the custom house.

---

[1] Upton, *Money in Politics*, p. 153.

VI.

THE public debt of the United States is twofold, viz.: interest bearing and non-interest bearing. This distinction is apt to be lost sight of in the failure to bear in mind the fact that all the paper money of the government, except the national bank notes, is evidence of a government debt pure and simple. The gold certificates and the silver certificates represent actual deposits of gold and silver coin, respectively, in the vaults of the Treasury. The currency certificates, in like manner, represent the deposit with the Treasury of legal tender notes ; while the legal tenders themselves, consisting of some $346,000,000 of greenbacks and of $151,000,000 of Sherman act Treasury notes, represent the government's promises to pay, based on its credit as a bank of issue, and having to secure them, respectively, a fluctuating "gold reserve" of nominally $100,000,000 and a mass of uncoined silver bullion in the Treasury. All of these various kinds of paper money are as much the government's obligations as are its bonds; though they are apt to be regarded by the general public merely as "money." They are all, either expressly, or by implication, payable in gold coin by virtue of the construction placed by the Treasury officials on the statutory declaration that "it is the established policy of the United States to maintain the two metals on a parity with each other upon the present legal ratio, or such ratio as may be provided by law." [1]

The national bank note is a limited liability obligation of the government, in that United States bonds are the basis of its security. But it is not so treated in the Treasury Department's dealings or statements; and for present purposes need not be considered in this connection.

The interest bearing debt of the United States is evidenced by its bonds; and in-

---

[1] Act, July 14, 1890, § 2.

cidentally, as indicative of how close is the connection between the government and the money market in this direction, as well as in that of the other paper currency of the country, it may be mentioned here that with the final payment of the national bond debt, the national banking system as at present constituted on its issue side must necessarily come to an end.[1]

The greater part of the interest bearing debt of the United States is like the greenbacks, a legacy of the Civil War.[2] The rapidity with which this stupendous war debt was created, reaching its climax in August, 1865, when the principal aggregated $2,844,649,626, has perhaps been only equalled in the history of national debts by the complementary ease and celerity with which it has been paid off and decreased.[3] It would be instructive and interesting to trace the history of this debt from its inception to its subsequent

---

[1] *Lalor's Cyclopædia*, article "United States Money."

[2] An analytical statement of the public debt is given in the *Statistical Abstract*, No. 15, issued by the Treasury Department.

[3] *Lalor's Cyclopædia*, article "Debts."

funding under act of the Congress, and
thence through its various phases of reduc-
tion down to 1893.[1]   But the purposes of
this volume only contemplate such reference to the bond debt of the government
as is necessary to an understanding of the
gold reserve and of the national bank note
circulation.

In 1880 the debt had been reduced to
$1,922,517,634; and a decade later to
$891,960,104.[2]   This amount in 1890 was
still further reduced in 1892 to $841,526,-
463,[3] and was in process of further reduc-
tion, when in 1894 a significant fact in
connection with its existence made itself
conspicuously apparent.   On January 17,
1894, after many fluctuations, the gold reserve held in the Federal Treasury for the
redemption of the greenbacks was reduced
to between $69,000,000 and $70,000,000.
The current expenses of the government
were in excess of the current receipts;
and, as a result, in order to build up the

---

[1] See H. C. Adams, *Public Debts*, p. 126, *et seq.*

[2] *Abstract of Eleventh Census*, p. 199.

[3] *Statistical Abstract U. S.* No. 15, p. 6.

gold reserve, bonds had to be issued and sold under the provisions of the act of January 1, 1875, known as the Resumption act. These bonds amounted to $50,-000,000, bore interest at five per cent., and were payable ten years from date.[1] They are said by the Secretary in his report to be "one of the three classes of bonds authorized by the act referred to."

This sale of bonds temporarily accomplished the purpose intended, but produced no permanent good results. Under the operation of the legal tenders which were redeemable in gold, because the word "coin" is so construed in the execution of the statutory financial policy enunciated by the Congress, and which are required in terms to be reissued when they come into the Treasury in order that there may be no "contraction of the currency,"[2] it was a very short time before the gold reserve again became diminished to such an extent as to warrant, in the opinion of the administration, the necessity of another $50,000,000

---

[1] *Report of the Secretary of the Treasury,* 1894, p. xlviii.
[2] Act, May 31, 1878.

issue of five per cent. bonds. This second
issue was disposed of in December, 1894,
and the proceeds of the sale covered into
the Treasury. In a very few weeks the
gold reserve had again sunk far below the
minimum recognized by the statute governing the reissue of gold certificates,[1] until
in February, 1895, it was down to the
$40,000,000 mark, — the lowest point
reached by it since 1879. Once more the
use of bonds was resorted to, but instead
of selling five per cent. bonds under the
act of 1875, as on the two preceding occasions, the government now bought from a
syndicate of American and European bankers 3,500,000 ounces of standard gold coin
of the United States, paying therefor with
bonds issued under the several acts of July
14, 1870, January 20, 1871, and January
14, 1875. These bonds bore interest at
four per cent., and were made payable "in
coin" at the government's option, after the
expiration of thirty years. The contract
for their purchase was held in abeyance by
the administration until the Congress had

---

[1] Act, July 12, 1882, § 12.

emphatically rejected a resolution authorizing a loan payable in express terms in gold
instead of "coin," which the contracting
syndicate had already agreed to take at a
less rate of interest than that which was
demanded in the "coin" bonds. In this
contract of purchase by the government of
gold for the further maintenance of its
Treasury reserve, the privilege was conceded the syndicate of bankers buying the
bonds therein provided for, to have the
refusal of all bonds to be issued thereafter
by the United States up to October 1,
1895.[1]

The fact that the price exacted for the
gold thus obtained was generally acknowl-
edged at the time to be excessive, and so
proven by the subsequent syndicate sales
of the bonds, added to the option conceded
to the syndicate in the contract, created
the almost inevitable impression upon the
public mind that the government felt itself
helpless in its efforts to protect the gold
reserve, and had in sheer desperation suc-

---

[1] The full text of this contract was published in the New
York daily papers of February 14, 1895.

cumbed to the repeated and successful onslaughts of the bankers, brokers, and money-dealers upon it. Perhaps, in all the financial history of the United States there exists no more pointed or conspicuous illustration of the truth of Mr. Bagehot's statement quoted on the title page of this volume,[1] than is afforded by the apparent helplessness of so magnificently wealthy a country as the United States in maintaining a comparatively small stock of gold in its National Treasury in the face of the organized attacks upon it.

The " gold reserve " has been described as an arbitrary balance carried on the books of the Treasury, unauthorized directly by law, and only recognized in the act which forbids the Secretary to reissue the redeemed gold certificates, when the reserve falls below one hundred million dollars. It has been not inaptly characterized as a barometer of public confidence; its rise and fall have been chronicled with assiduous and often sensational attention and detail by the newspaper press; and the financial and business temper of the country

---

[1] *Lombard Street* (American ed.), chap. iv., p. 101.

has been so affected by its shifting conditions that enterprise and credit have alike wavered in fluctuant unison with its variations. It had its origin in the operations of the Treasury under the provisions of the Resumption act, passed by the Congress in 1875. The object of that act was to redeem the greenbacks when presented at the Sub-Treasury in New York City in coin. Secretary Sherman, without authority of law, construed "coin" to mean gold; and accumulated prior to January, 1879, the date at which the act was to go into effect, $135,000,000 of gold coin and bullion in the Treasury for the purposes of redemption.[1] In a letter to the Senate on May 19, 1879, he stated that the Treasury had been called on to redeem only $4,133,513 of greenbacks,—less, as a matter of fact, than it had received in gold in exchange for United States notes; and that the "coin reserve" had been increased to $138,000,-000, or about forty per cent. of the then outstanding legal tenders.[2] The indications

---

[1] Upton, *Money in Politics*, p. 154.

[2] "The Future of Resumption," *North Am. Rev.*, Aug., 1879.

of the success of resumption and of the permanent maintenance of the government's paper on an equality with gold seemed most promising. But the prohibition in the act of May 31, 1878, of the retirement of the redeemed notes, the accumulation of standard silver dollars in the Treasury under the Bland-Allison act of February 28, 1878, and the issue of the legal tender coin notes under the Sherman law of July 14, 1890, have concurred to place obstacles apparently insurmountable in the way of a successful administration of the currency of the country by the general government.

Says the writer of the article on "The Future of Resumption," published in the *North American Review* for August of the year when the act went into operation, and which, read in the light of subsequent events, seems pregnant of prophesy :

"By the redemption law as Judge Edmunds intended it, the notes of the government were to be paid, retired, cancelled, destroyed. They were to pass forever from the currency to be replaced by gold. The government by the operation of this law was gradually to take its heavy and unsteady

hand off the financial affairs of the country ; it was
to withdraw from the exercise of the function of
currency making, which had become so dangerous
and had worked so much mischief ; it was to leave
the business of the country to regulate itself by the
laws which are higher than the laws of Congress,
simpler and far safer ; in a word, the forced war
loan, which had been levied in the form of legal
tender notes, was to be paid ; and the government
was to leave the business community the freedom
which was its right." [1]

No financial declaration of independence
has ever been or can ever be penned in
America with more of sovereign freedom
and sovereign truth in its lines than are
contained in this utterance. But the " heavy
and unsteady hand " reasserted itself between the enactment of the Resumption
act in 1875, and the date fixed for resumption to begin in 1879. On May 31,
1878, the Congress enacted the law forbidding the cancellation and retirement of the
greenbacks and compelling their reissue ;
and thus constituting the United States
Treasury a bank of indefinite paper issue,
made the government legal tenders and the

---

[1] *North Amer. Review*, August, 1879, p. 189.

gold reserve " a perpetual element and the controlling one in the currency."

In 1885 the gold reserve fell to some $114,000,000 ; and the then Treasurer of the United States called conspicuous public notice to its precarious existence with the announcement that in his opinion the further depletion of the fund would imperil the maintenance of gold payments. A well informed writer on contemporary finance makes the assertion that " a similar announcement by Secretary Foster in 1893, when the fund was $108,000,000 precipitated the crash of that year." [1]

In 1879 the Secretary of the Treasury in his annual report called the attention of the Congress to the " gold reserve " fund and " recommended that to avoid all uncertainty this fund be specifically defined and set apart for the redemption of United States notes, and that the notes redeemed be reissued only in exchange for or purchase of coin or bullion." [2] But the Congress said neither Yea or Nay; and the gold reserve, carried as a part of the ordi-

---

[1] Matthew Marshall in *N. Y. Sun*, Feb. 11, 1895.

[2] Upton, *Money in Politics*, p. 155.

nary Treasury balance, remains, in the opinion of Mr. Upton, himself a prominent Ex-Assistant Secretary of the Treasury, subject to the warrant of the Secretary of the Treasury at any time and " perhaps for any purpose."

The expense of maintaining the gold reserve, as shown in an " accurate statement obtained from the Treasury,"[1] by the Comptroller of the Currency, during its existence from January 1, 1879, to January 1, 1895, has been as follows :

Principal of bonds sold for resumption purposes :

Sold in 1877 and 1878........	$ 95,500,000
Sold in 1894............................	100,000,000
" " 1895............................	62,400,000

$257,900,000

Interest at 4 per cent. on the average amount of the free gold in the Treasury from January 1, 1879, to January 1, 1895.....$ 93,440,000

$351,340,000

Interest from January 1, 1895, to July 1, 1907, on $30,500,000 4 per cent. bonds of 1907	$ 15,250,000
Interest from January 1, 1895, to February 1, 1904, on $100,000,000 5 per cent. bonds	· 45,416,666
Interest from February 1, 1895, to February 1, 1925, on $62,400,000 4 per cent. bonds	74,880,000

$486,886,666

---

[1] J. H. Eckels, " The Business World vs. The Politicians," *The Forum* for March, 1895.

VII.

GOLD COINS; THE SILVER DOLLAR; AND SUBSIDIARY COINAGE.

SINCE 1873, when by act of the Congress the mints of the United States were closed to the legal tender silver dollar by the omission from the statute of any provision for its further coinage, "the battle of the standards" has been waged with a fervor unparalleled in the history of politico-economic controversy in America since the famous removal of the deposits from the second Bank of the United States by President Jackson. The earlier currency struggles concerned themselves chiefly with the government's connection with a national bank; and the metallic question seldom arose prominently save in the aspect of "hard money" as contradistinguished from the bank issues.[1]

---

[1] Cluskey, *Political Text Book*, article, " Independent Treasury.'

From 1814 to 1834 gold and silver as a currency were practically unknown in the United States ; the notes of the Bank of the United States serving as a circulating medium acceptable everywhere.[1] From 1834 to the passage of the Mint act of 1873 silver commanded a high price relative to gold. A silver dollar was worth more than a gold dollar; and gold (that is, the gold eagle, half eagle and quarter eagle, up to 1849, and the same gold coins, together with the gold dollar and double eagle, after 1849) had been practically the only coin money of the Treasury in circulation in the United States.[2] The reason given for the existence of this state of facts by the gold mono-metallists is that the value of silver in the silver dollar was more than the value of gold in the gold dollar; and that the silver dollars, under the influence of the financial force known to political economists and financiers as Gresham's Law (which is, in effect, that an inferior currency, circulating on an equality with a superior currency,

---

[1] *Lalor's Cyclopædia*, article, "Bank Controversies."
[2] Sherwood, *The History and Theory of Money*, chap. vi.

7

tends ultimately to drive the latter out of circulation), left the country, or ceased to circulate as soon as coined and issued.

The originators of the legislation of 1873 which closed the Federal mints to the free coinage of the standard silver dollar, and expressly declared that the gold dollar should be thenceforward what the silver dollar had always nominally been theretofore, namely, the standard of value,[1] were undoubtedly gold-monometallists. They considered that it was useless to continue the coinage of a silver dollar which, owing to the high price of silver, failed to circulate; and believed that in enacting this legislation the Federal government was keeping abreast of the financial policy of the civilized commercial world. The International Monetary Conference, held in Paris in 1867, had enunciated as the fundamental principle essential to universal coinage, that there should be a general adoption by the commercial nations of the world of the single gold standard.[2] England had adopted this

---

[1] Sherwood, *The History and Theory of Money*, p. 165. Henry Loomis Nelson, *Bimetallism in History*, p. 10.

[2] Ehrich, *The Question of Silver*, p. 17. R. W. Hughes *The Currency Question*, chap. xii.

policy in 1816 under the administration of Lord Liverpool; Germany had in 1871 begun preparations for establishing the gold standard; and in 1876 France and the Latin Union, following the examples set by such powerful nations, ceased the free and unlimited coinage of legal tender silver.

The price of silver fell; until in 1876[1] a fierce outcry went up against the Congress, which the advocates of silver alleged had in 1873 "secretly demonetized" that metal at the behest of British capital.

It was charged by the silver advocates, and was asserted later on the floor of the United States Senate, that English influences had sent emissaries to this country to buy legislation in favor of gold, and that Ernest Seyd,[2] an eminent English authority on finance, had come to Washington, and assisted in the framing of the Coinage act in question ; and that through his efforts the standard silver dollar had been eliminated from the list of coins therein provided for.[3]

---

[1] Nelson, *Bimetallism in History*, p. 11. For an account of the causes of the decline of silver see Prof. J. Lawrence Laughlin's *History of Bimetallism in U. S.*

[2] Ehrich, *The Question of Silver*, p. 50.

[3] Speech of Hon. Jno. W. Daniel, U. S. Sen., May 22, 1890.

7

The opponents of the free coinage of silver replied to this charge that as matter of history, the act of 1873 for regulating the coinage was framed by the Hon. John Jay Knox, then deputy Comptroller of the Treasury, in 1870; that it was sent to the Congress by Secretary of the Treasury Boutwell, with Mr. Knox's report expressly explaining the reason for the discontinuance of the coinage of the silver dollar, then worth a premium of 7 per cent. in gold ; and that between that time and 1873 it was printed thirteen times by order of the Congress, and once by the commissioners revising the United States statutes.

While on the one hand it is true that the bill was discussed on the floor of the Congress, and that the reports of the debates show that the discontinuance of the coinage of the standard silver dollar was especially adverted to in the discussion,[1] there can be little doubt, that, owing to the peculiar

---

[1] Nelson, *Bimetallism in History*, p. 10 ; Wilson, *Congressional Government* (10th edition), p. 185 ; Hon. Jno. Sherman in U. S. Senate, May 22, 1890 ; Ehrich, *The Question of Silver*, p. 18 ; Upton, *Money in Politics*, ch. xx.

committee legislation of the Congress, or to the then general indifference of the Congress to the money question, or for some other specific reason, this feature of the bill was either not understood, or not maturely considered by the body enacting it; for President Grant himself has said that he signed the bill without knowing that its most important effect was to demonetize silver.[1] But from the date of the passage of the act of 1873, up to the present time, there has, on the other hand, been no satisfactory proof adduced that its enactment was procured by indirect or improper means, or that the omission of any provision for the further coinage of the silver dollar was purposely concealed by its originators. It is more than probable that the fact that paper money being the sole currency then in existence, and resumption apparently many years off, the average member of the Congress thought little and knew less in 1873 of the relations of gold and silver to each other as money.

The general impression prevails that

[1] *Memoirs of Thurlow Weed*, vol. ii., chap. 39.

when by the Mint act of 1873 the standard silver dollar was dropped from the
list of United States coins, the government
mints were at once opened for the free and
unlimited coinage of gold. This, however,
is not true. The gold dollar was by that
act made in law the standard of value, as it
had been in fact since 1834 ; but a fixed
charge was established by the statute itself,
for converting gold bullion into coin ;[1] and
it was not until the passage of the Resumption act in 1875 that gold coinage was
made free.[2]

From the foundation of the government
until February 12, 1873, the silver dollar
of 371¼ grains of pure silver was the nominal unit of value in the United States, and
its coinage was free at the mints ; and when
coined it had full legal tender value.[3] The
intrinsic amount of pure silver in the standard silver dollar has never varied. The
amount of alloy and the ratio of its value

---

[1] *Rev. Statutes U. S.* § 3524.

[2] H. C. Adams, *Public Debts*, p. 201.

[3] An instructive and interesting article on the "Standard of
Value," by Prof. Simon Newcomb, may be found in *North
American Review* for September, 1879.

to that of the gold coins have varied with legislation; but in the inflexible unchangeableness of its intrinsic silver it has been unvarying, at least, in all that time as a "standard of value." As has been stated, from 1834 to 1873, the silver dollar had been at a premium. The act of 1834 had changed the ratio between the metals from 15 grains of silver to 1 grain of gold to that of 16 to 1, contributing thereby to the circumstances which put silver at a premium. Writers on the subject assert that for this reason the alleged demonetization of silver by the Mint Act of 1873 was the "mere formal declaration of a fact";[1] the fact being that it had been practically demonetized in 1834 by the change of ratio and increase in value. The discovery of gold in California in 1849, and the passage of the act of 1853, reducing the amount of silver in the fractional currency and making it "token money," contributed later to strengthening gold monometallism in the United States.[2]

---

[1] Nelson, *Bimetallism in History*, p. 10.
[2] Nelson, *Bimetallism in History*, p. 10.

From the foundation of the government down to 1877, only $8,031,238 standard legal tender silver dollars had ever been coined and sent out from the Treasury. Of this $8,031,238, in the forty-six years that elapsed from the coinage of the first silver dollar up to 1840, only $1,501,822 had been coined, the coinage of silver dollars having been wholly suspended for thirty years from 1806 by executive order.[1] From 1873 to 1878 none were coined. During that time the country was not only in fact, but in law also, on a gold basis. From 1878, when the Bland-Allison act restored the coinage of the standard silver dollar, up to 1894, $421,776,408 were coined. The "dollar of the daddies" was the slang war-cry of the free silver advocates from 1876 on ; but the "dollar of the daddies" was a pigmy in comparison with its gigantic descendant of 1878. Of this large number of silver dollars, the greater proportion remained in the Treasury vaults, silver certificates being issued against them. Up to July 1893 not more than sixty millions of

---

[1] *Lalor's Cyclopædia*, article, "Coinage."

these coined standard silver dollars had
ever been put into actual circulation. The
advocates of the free and unlimited coinage
of silver, when confronted with the comparatively small amount of standard silver dollars coined between 1792 and 1873, reply
that though only eight millions of silver
dollars were put into circulation in that
time, ninety-seven millions had been coined
into dimes, quarters, and half dollars. To
this, the monometallist's answer in the discussion is that while this is true, the ninety-
seven millions of silver coinage was subsidiary coinage and did not possess full
legal tender capacity; and that no single
standard gold advocate objects, now, or
ever has objected, to the indefinite coinage
of such silver money.

The legal tender quality of the silver
dollar that had been coined up to the date
of the passage of the Coinage act of 1873
had not been taken from it by that act ; but
the revisers of the United States statutes,
whose revision became law, June 20, 1874,
superseding all pre-existing laws, made all
the silver coins of the United States a

legal tender for payments not exceeding five dollars; and while the failure to make the silver dollar an exception, and the consequent destruction of its full legal tender significance, was evidently an oversight, the act operated to make all silver dollars coined prior to 1873 legal tender only in sums not exceeding five dollars.[1] This error was remedied, however, by the Bland-Allison act of 1878, which provided for the restoration of the full legal tender quality to all of the silver dollars theretofore coined by the United States, of like weight and fineness with those whose coinage was provided for under that act, so that now all the silver dollars of the government which ever possessed the legal tender feature, possess it to an unqualified extent.

The Bland-Allison act became a law on February 28, 1879, by the passage over the veto of President Hayes. In its original form, as it came from the House of Representatives in the fall of 1877, it was a free coinage bill. In the Senate the free coinage feature was eliminated and it passed that

---

[1] Upton, *Money in Politics*, p. 207.

body as amended by Senator Allison, becoming a law in the manner stated.[1]

Once more the fires of wrath leaped up
between the "gold bugs" and "silver
lunatics," as the contending factions respectively dubbed each other. The former had
had their day after the passage of the
Coinage act of 1873. It was now their
turn to shout "fraud!" They said that
"the whole thing was a job from the beginning; that there was nothing in the currency or finances of the country calling for
such an enormous coinage of silver, or for
any issue at all of the piece in question;
that the sole motive of the mine owners,
who were the originators of the project,
was to secure a steady and active market
for a large portion of their product; and
that they found as allies a considerable
body of dealers, who hoped to profit from
an inflated currency; and they forced the
measure through both houses of Congress by
the use of such means as have been plied for
many years in behalf of corrupt measures."[2]

[1] Ehrich, *The Question of Silver*, p. 22. Nelson, *Bimetallism in History*, p. 12.

[2] *N. Y. Journal of Commerce*, April 27, 1889.

Whatever the circumstances may have been under which the compromise Bland-Allison act was passed, it is as little probable that its passage was accomplished by the means above charged, as that such influences were used to destroy the provision for silver coinage at the time of the enactment of the famous Mint act of 1873. As little pleasing as the Bland-Allison act was to the gold faction, it was hardly less so to the free silver advocates, the gravamen of whose complaint against it was that it contained, in the provision that the silver dollars coined under it should be "legal tender at their nominal value, for all debts and dues, public and private, except where otherwise expressly stipulated in the contract," authority and sanction for taking notes, bonds, mortgages, and contracts of debt generally, payable in gold.[1]

The act of February 28, 1878, restored the standard silver dollar to the list of coins, but it did not provide for its free and unlimited coinage at the mints. It forced the United States Treasury into the

[1] W. H. Harvey, *Coin's Financial School*, p. 30.

extension of its banking business in another direction than that in which the greenback legislation had compelled it, by requiring the Secretary to buy not less than two millions nor more than four million dollars' worth of silver bullion per month, and to coin this bullion into silver dollars, which should be full legal tender at "their nominal value." Under the provisions of this act the holder of ten or more of these silver dollars might exchange them for silver certificates, which are receivable for customs taxes, and all public dues; but are not themselves legal tender. The silver certificates are discussed more at length in a subsequent chapter.[1]

During the agitation of the "free coinage" question by the Congress, resulting in the passage of the Bland-Allison act, the Senate passed a resolution declaring that the United States Government might legally redeem its bonds in silver dollars. European holders began thereupon to throw their bonds on the market;[2] and from that

---

[1] *Post*, chap. x.
[2] Nelson, *Bimetallism in History*, p. 13.

date to the present time the "silver scare" has seldom failed to precipitate an "unloading" of American securities by foreign holders, and a run on the Treasury gold reserve.

The silver dollars coined under the Bland-Allison act were not popular. The clearing-houses refused to accept them in settlement of balances, as heretofore narrated; and legislation by the Congress to compel such acceptance has been silently ignored or disregarded. In order to promote their circulation the government provided free transportation of the silver dollars; it ceased the reissuing of greenbacks in sums less than five dollars; and it reduced the denominations of the silver certificates to one, two, and five dollars. While the low denominations of certificates proved equally acceptable to the people as any other paper notes of like amounts, the silver dollar itself has steadily refused to circulate as such, except to a limited degree.

On July 14, 1890, the Sherman act was passed by the Congress. It was amenda-

tory of the act of 1878; and like it a compromise measure.[1] The Senate, which in
1878 had differed with the House in being
opposed to the free coinage of silver, had
become in favor of it in 1890, and would
have made the act of 1890 a free coinage
law but for the action of the conferees of
the House. Not being able to make it a
free coinage law, the Senate concurred with
the House in doing what was perhaps
worse than enacting free coinage, viz.,
giving the legal tender attribute in time of
profound peace and without necessity to
the paper notes issued under it. The act
of July 14, 1890, directed the Secretary of
the Treasury to buy four and a half million
ounces of silver per month at the current
market price, (but not to exceed a fixed
limit to this price) and to issue legal tender
Treasury notes in payment therefor, which
notes are redeemable in gold or silver
coin at the option of the government. The
act provided further that the coinage of
silver dollars authorized by the Bland-
Allison act should cease after July 1, 1891,

---

[1] Ehrich, *The Question of Silver*, p. 24.

except as such coinage should be necessary for the redemption of the Treasury notes issued under it. The statutory declaration that it is "the established policy of the United States to maintain the two metals on a parity with each other upon the present legal ratio," as construed by the Treasury officials, has resulted in the redemption of the Sherman Treasury notes in gold, except as to some four millions of these notes that were redeemed with silver dollars, coined for the purpose, and after redemption were cancelled and retired by Secretary Carlisle in 1893 and 1894. This statutory declaration of the government's "established policy" appears as such for the first time in the act of 1890. The Resumption act of 1875 was prepared by Senator Edmunds of Vermont; though in the altered and reconstructed form in which it became a law, it was the work of a political party caucus of the Congress.[1] It provided that the legal tenders should be redeemed in "coin." As a matter of fact they have, since 1879, when the Resump-

---

[1] Upton, *Money in Politics*, p. 147.

tion act went into effect, been continuously redeemed in gold, save in the instance mentioned above, "solely because the Secretary, in the exercise of a discretion nowhere distinctly conferred upon him" by law until 1890, has chosen so to do.[1]

The Sherman act, under which a tremendous mass of silver bullion was accumulated in the vaults of the Treasury at a net loss of between fifty and sixty millions of dollars to the government, incident to the steady decrease in the value of silver, and by the provisions of which legal tender Treasury notes to the amount of more than $150,000,000 were put into circulation, based on the depreciated silver bullion, is believed by many financiers and men of affairs to have contributed largely to the precipitation of the panic of 1893. The struggle of the silver advocates, though

[1] "The Future of Resumption," *North American Review* for August, 1879.

A remarkable illustration of the "unsteadiness of the hand" with which the Congress regulates the currency is the fact that in October, 1877, a special session saw introduced in one day thirteen different bills for the repeal of the Resumption act, one of which actually passed the House the following month.—Upton, *Money in Politics*, chap. xvii.

8

never achieving free coinage, had been so determined and had apparently accomplished so much in the direction of a rehabilitation of silver, in spite of the actual fall in market prices, that the holders of American securities in Europe again became alarmed. The exports of gold and gold bullion, which had been between thirty-four and thirty-five millions of dollars in 1888, had grown in 1893 to nearly eighty millions. Not only did the exportation of gold indicate its departure from circulation, but the falling off in gold payments to the government on account of customs duties emphasized this disappearance in another way. In January 1890, 92.6 per cent. of the government's customs dues were paid in gold; while in January, 1893, 8.9 per cent only were paid in gold.[1]

On the other hand the advocates of the free and unlimited coinage of silver have contended no less earnestly that the panic was a thing of steady growth, reaching its ultimate climax in 1893; the result of the demonetization of silver and of the in-

---

[1] Nelson, *Bimetallism in History*, page 14.

creased value of gold; of lowered prices
and enlarged difficulty on the part of the
debtor class to obtain relief; and that the
severe stringency and the depressed condition of business which succeeded the
panic, continuing so long thereafter, was
attributable, in degree at least, to the failure
of the Congress on repealing the Sherman
act in November, 1893, to provide for the
future free coinage of the legal tender
silver dollar.[1]

The development of the coinage system
of the United States has been of gradual
growth. It was while Robert Morris, the
great Superintendent of Finance of the
Continental Congress, was in charge of the
Board of Treasury, that the subject of the
coinage was first considered by the Congress. In a minute and detailed communi-
cation to that body he recommended the
establishment of a mint, and outlined a
plan of coinage. Mr. Jefferson and Gouv-
erneur Morris also contributed to the

---

[1] An able and instructive presentation of this side of the
question may be found in the speech of Hon. Jno. W. Daniel,
in the Senate, September 14, 1893.

general scheme.[1] It was in compliance with Morris' suggestion in connection with his mint scheme that the Spanish silver dollar was adopted by the Continental Congress in 1785 as the standard of value, having been-first so adopted by the colony of Virginia in 1645, and subsequently by the other colonies.[2] In the same statute making the Spanish milled dollar the standard, provision was made for the decimal system of currency, in accordance with the suggestion of Jefferson.

The United States Mint was established by act of April, 1792, under authority of article 1, section 8 of the Constitution, which vests in the Congress power to coin money and regulate the value thereof and of foreign coins. Its author was Alexander Hamilton, first Secretary of the Treasury under Washington, who, at the request of the House of Representatives prepared and submitted an elaborate scheme for a government mint and for its future coinage operations in his " Report on the Establish-

---

[1] *Lalor's Cyclopædia*, article, " American Finance."
[2] Upton, *Money in Politics*, chap. iii., *Id.* chap. vii.

ment of a Mint," [1] a finance paper as remarkable in its way as is the "Report on a National Bank" by the same master-hand. The act of 1792 provided that the mint should be located at the seat of government, which was then at Philadelphia. When the seat of government was removed to Washington, the Congress directed that the mint should remain in Philadelphia until March 4, 1801. This period was extended by subsequent legislation from time to time, until 1828, when the location was made permanent in Philadelphia until otherwise ordered by the Congress. All the coinage of the government up to 1835 was done at the Philadelphia mint. In that year branch mints were established for the convenient coinage of gold and silver in or adjacent to their respective localities as then known. By the Coinage act of 1873, each of the branch mints was made an independent mint under the control of an officer created by that statute called the Director of the Mint.[2]

---

[1] *Finance Reports*, vol. i., p. 133, *et seq.*
Lalor's Cyclopædia, article, " Coinage."

The mints are located in the cities of Philadelphia, San Francisco, New Orleans, Carson, and Denver; and there are assay offices of the government at New York, Boise City, and Charlotte, N. C.

In the act of April, 1792, authority was given for the coinage of the gold eagle, half eagle, and quarter eagle. In 1794 the first silver dollar was actually coined, and in 1795 the first gold eagle.[1] It was not until after the passage of the act of March 3, 1849, incident to the discovery of gold in California, that the gold dollar came into existence. By act of September 26, 1890, the coinage of the gold dollar ceased. It was never by law the standard of value in the United States until it was expressly declared to be so by the coinage act of 1873; and for only about forty years of the Republic has it had an actual existence.

The original Mint act of 1792 also authorized the coinage of the silver dollar, half dollar, quarter dollar, dime- and half dime. By this act the free coinage of both gold and silver was authorized at the ratio

---

[1] W. G. Sumner, *American Currency*, p. 60.

of 15 to 1, and each was made unlimited legal tender. In 1834, as has been stated, the ratio was changed to 16 to 1, or, to be exact, to 15.988 to 1. This ratio is that which now exists, and has been preserved in all coinage subsequent to its establishment. By the act of January 18, 1837, the standard for gold and silver coins, and their several weights, were fixed; the gold eagle, half eagle, and quarter eagle were made legal tender; and all the coins that had been legal tender under the Coinage act of 1834 had their legal tender quality continued.

The dollar is the nominal unit of value in the Federal decimal system of coinage; and thus, under the primary coinage act, while the coinage system was bimetallic, the standard unit was nominally the silver dollar, as it continued to be until 1873. The law of 1873 expressly declared that the gold dollar should be the standard unit of value; and there has been no change in the standard since the enactment of that law.[1] As a matter of fact, however,

---

[1] Sherwood, *History and Theory of Money*, p. 165 ; Upton, *Money in Politics*, p. 40.

since the act of September 26, 1890, suspending the coinage of the gold dollar, as stated, no gold dollars have been coined for circulation by the United States Government.

Since the passage of the Sherman act of 1890, that law has been the only one by virtue of which the continued coinage of the standard silver dollar was possible. The entire amount of silver purchased by the government under the provisions of the " purchasing clause " of that act, aggregated 168,674,682.53 ounces, costing $155,-931,002.25, the "coining value" of which in silver dollars was $218,084,438. Yet of this tremendous quantity of bullion there had been coined up to November 1, 1894, only $38,531,143 such dollars.[1] The act itself provided that the Secretary of the Treasury should coin two million ounces per month into standard silver dollars until July 1, 1891, after which time he should coin as much as might be necessary to provide for the redemption of the Treasury

---

[1] Report of the Director of the Mint, in the *Banker's Magazine* for April, 1895.

notes issued under the act, and that any
gain or seigniorage arising therefrom should
be accounted for and paid into the Treasury.[1] On November 1, 1893, the "purchasing clause" of the act was repealed,
and the further purchase of silver bullion
thereunder ceased.

"Since November 1, 1893, there has been coined
from silver bullion purchased under the act of July
14, 1890, 3,594,489 standard silver dollars. The
cost of the bullion contained in this number of
dollars was $2,434,397.79, and this sum has been used
or held for the redemption of Treasury notes issued
in payment for bullion contained in such dollars,
and the difference, $1,160,091.21 (the seigniorage),
has been paid into the Treasury and made available for use in payment on account of current
expenses of the government. To the extent of the
seigniorage is the number of silver dollars available
for general circulation increased."[2]

Under the act of March 3, 1849, the
coinage of the double eagle, or twenty-dol-
lar gold piece, was authorized; and under
that of March 3, 1851, the coinage of the

---

[1] Act, July 14, 1890, § 3.
[2] Letter of Hon. R. E. Preston, Director of the Mint, to
the Author, April 26, 1895.

silver three-cent piece, the weight and fineness of the latter being established in the
act. By the act of February 21, 1853, the
three-dollar gold piece was authorized, and
its further coinage repealed by that of
September 26, 1890.[1] The act of February
12, 1873, heretofore spoken of as "demon-
etizing" or discontinuing the coinage of
the standard silver dollar, also discontinued
the coinage of the silver half dime and
three-cent piece, and authorized the coinage of the "trade dollar" of 420 grains of
silver, 378 grains pure. This coin was provided for in the act in response to the
unanimous resolution of the Legislature of
California, presented to the United States
Senate by a Senator from that state.[2] It
was intended to supersede the Mexican
silver dollar, then in common use on the
Pacific slope, and largely used as a medium
of exchange with China and the other
nations of the East. By a mistake in the
preparation of the act, a legal tender qual-

---

[1] John S. Hanson, *Gold and Silver*, p. 4.
[2] Hon. John Sherman in U. S. Senate, May 22, 1890.

ity up to five dollars was given it, as in the case of the subsidiary silver coins therein provided for; but the mistake was corrected by subsequent legislation, which deprived it in any amount of a legal tender attribute.[1] The coinage of the trade dollar ceased in 1878, except for specimen pieces, its brief five years' existence having demonstrated it to be impracticable for the purposes had in view in its coinage, although it contained more silver than the standard silver dollar. It was never popular and was almost always current for less than its nominal value.

Under the act of March 3, 1875, the silver twenty-cent piece was coined. It was discontinued by legislative enactment in May, 1878.

All fractional silver coins of the United States, known as "subsidiary coins," are legal tender to the amount of five dollars.[2] Since 1853 the subsidiary silver coins have been what is technically known as "token

---

[1] Nelson, *Bimetallism in History*, p. 10.
[2] Act Feb. 21, 1873, § 15.

currency," that is, coins which are not intrinsically worth their face value.[1] They
have been coined since that time by the
government for its own account out of
bullion purchased by it for the purpose.

---

[1] Act Feb. 21, 1853. Sherwood, *History and Theory of
Money*, p. 164.

VIII.

UNITED STATES NOTES, OR "GREENBACKS";
POSTAL-CURRENCY, AND FRACTIONAL CUR-
RENCY.

THE United States Treasury note, known
to history as the greenback, was issued
by authority of the act of the Congress of
February 25, 1862. It is an inconvertible
paper currency,[1] reciting in terms that it is
a legal tender at its face value for all debts,
public and private, except duties on imports, and interest on the public debt; and
is made payable to the bearer, but not on
demand, nor at any fixed time. It is a
significant fact that the greenback is the
only unlimited legal tender issued by the
government which is not and never has
been receivable in payment of customs duties;[2] and in this respect it conspicuously

---

[1] Francis A. Walker, *Money*, chap. xvi., p. 374.
[2] J. J. Knox, *United States Notes*, p. 154.

differs from the Treasury legal tender note issued under the provisions of the Sherman act of 1890. It was an experiment in finance, having its origin in the exigencies of war. Mr. Francis A. Walker speaks of it as "a measure of resource," and says that the recognized alternative was the sale of the government bonds below par for gold.[1] Its author was the Hon. Elbridge G. Spaulding, a member of the Ways and Means Committee of the Congress which enacted the statute.[2] The unexpected and unforeseen source from which it is possible under congressional government for currency measures of the most radical character to emanate, is shown in the fact that the greenback was originated, not by the committee on Banking and Currency, but by the great tax-levying committee of the Ways and Means.

The most conspicuous, though apparently unwilling advocate and supporter of

---

[1] Walker, *Money*, p. 369; Upton, *Money in Politics*, chap. xii.

[2] W. G. Sumner, *American Currency*, p. 197. *Appleton's Biog. Cycloped.*, Article " E. G. Spaulding."

the greenback legislation was the Hon. Salmon P. Chase, Mr. Lincoln's first Secretary of the Treasury, who, when he became Chief-Justice of the United States, delivered the opinion of the Court[1] in the case of *Hepburn vs. Griswold*, declaring the legal tender feature of the greenback to be unconstitutional and the act itself invalid. Subsequently, the United States Supreme Court in the *Legal Tender Cases*,[2] reversed its position on this momentous question; but Chase maintained his views as first expressed from the bench, delivering a strong dissenting opinion. In speaking of the position taken by Mr. Chase in this matter, Mr. Justice Field said that Chase preferred to preserve his integrity as a judicial officer, rather than his consistency as a statesman.[3] In his dissenting opinion in the *Legal Tender Cases*, the Chief-Justice said that the Secretary of the Treasury was extremely averse to the legal tender clause

---

[1] 8 Wallace, 603.

[2] 12 Wallace, 457.

[3] W. D. Dabney, " Paper Money," *7th Reports Virginia State Bar Association*, p. 210 ; See Justice Field's dissenting opinion in Juilliard v. Greenman, 110 *U. S. Reports*, p. 421.

of the act, but was very solicitous for the passage of the bill; and was finally persuaded to take the risk of making the notes legal tender rather than lose the use of them in the emergency then existing.[1] The legal tender clause was apparently an afterthought, subsequent to the preparation of the bill, for it did not appear in the original draft.

Up to the time of the legislation of 1862, it had been generally considered and conceded, as Chase deemed it in his capacity of Judge, to be unconstitutional for the United States to issue bills of credit or notes, payable on presentation, and without interest,[2] and in the almost seventy-five years that had elapsed since the adoption of the Federal Constitution none had been issued with the exception of one put forth in 1815.[3] This Treasury note of early years is said to have been very similar to the long subsequent greenback, save in that it lacked the legal tender quality. The similarity con-

---

[1] Upton, *Money in Politics*, p. 78.

[2] Mr. Justice Field's dissenting opinion in Juilliard vs. Greenman, 110 *U. S. Reports*, 421.

[3] Upton, *Money in Politics*, p. 76.

sisted in the facts that it was payable to bearer, that it passed by mere delivery, that it bore no interest, that it had no fixed time of payment, and that it was convertible into government bonds.

During the war of 1812, the proposition had been offered in the House of Repre- sentatives to make Treasury issues a legal tender in the payment of private debts; but the House refused even to consider this suggestion. [1]

What were known as Treasury notes had been issued by the government at different times, beginning as far back as 1812 ; but they were a species of government bond, bearing interest, maturing usually after a brief stated period, and without the legal tender quality ; the exception to the general character of the species of notes described being a part of the issue of 1815, which were of less denominations than $100, and intended . to supplement the depreciated bank notes then in use, and whose peculiar characteristics have been just above

---

[1] *Annals 13th Congress,* 1814, 1815, vol. iii., p. 557, cited in Hon. W. D. Dabney's " Paper Currency," *7th Va. Bar Asso. Reports,* 1894.

9

described as so closely resembling those of
the greenback. The interest bearing government notes were created for the convenience
of the Treasury in its fiscal operations, and
were in no sense intended for general circulation as currency. The greatest amount
ever outstanding was about $10,000,000,
though their aggregate issues reached the
sum of $50,000,000.[1] They were generally
of large denominations, and were not receivable in payment of private debts, save
at the option of the creditor. Some were
convertible into United States securities;
some were payable at the Treasury in
currency; and some were not payable at
all in money, but were only receivable for
certain public dues. These interest-bearing
notes, in the nature of government bonds,
being evidences of loans made to the
United States, were issued at four different
periods in the history of the country; viz.:
the War of 1812; the financial crisis of
1837; the Mexican War; and the financial
crisis of 1857.[2]

---

[1] Upton, *Money in Politics*, p. 53.

[2] *Lalor's Cyclopædia*, article " American Finance " ; Knox,
United States Notes, ch. v. ; Upton, *Money in Politics*, chap. x.

But there had been, up to the passage of the act of 1862, no legal tender for private debts in the United States except "specie"; and, in fact, the only paper currency, in the proper acceptation of the term and used generally as a circulating medium, had been that issued by private corporations and payable on demand in coin.[1]

Under the act of 1862 the issue of one hundred and fifty million dollars of greenbacks was authorized; and further issues of one hundred and fifty millions more by each of the two subsequent acts of July 11, 1862, and March 3, 1863.

The issues under act of February 25, 1862, were in denominations of not less than five dollars. Of the issues under the act of July 11, 1862, $35,000,000 were authorized to be in denominations of less than five dollars, the Secretary of the Treasury giving as a reason that "since the United States notes are made a legal tender and maintained nearly at the par of gold by the provision for their conversion into bonds bearing six per cent. interest

---

[1] Richardson, *The National Banks*, p. 22.

payable in coin, it is not easy to see why
small notes may not be issued as widely as
large ones."[1] The highest amount of greenbacks ever actually issued was that outstanding in June, 1864, aggregating a little
less than the authorized four hundred and
fifty millions.[2] In December, 1865,[3] the
Congress by resolution approved the plan
of Secretary McCulloch for retiring the
greenbacks. This resolution was passed
under a suspension of the rules, and by the
tremendous majority in the House of 146
ayes to 6 nays.[4] The work was systemati-
cally begun, and was well under way when
the stringency of the money market and
the fall of prices caused the Congress on
February 4, 1868,[5] to repeal the act of
December, 1865, which had directed the
retirement of the legal tenders.[6] By the
withdrawals under the last named act the
greenbacks had been reduced to $356,000,-

[1] Upton, *Money in Politics*, ch. xiii.
[2] Upton, *Money in Politics*, ch. xiii.
[3] Act, December 18, 1865.
[4] Upton, *Money in Politics*, p. 128.
[5] Knox, *United States Notes*, p. 140.
[6] Walker, *Money*, p. 374.

000. Professor Sumner notes the fact that January, 1868, just prior to the repeal of the act of 1865, was "the turning point at which the contraction of the legal tender notes met the expansion of the national bank note circulation," the bank issues at that date standing at $294,000,000. As shown by the report of the Secretary of the Treasury in December, 1894, the amount of the general stock of greenbacks in the United States on November 1, 1894, was $346,681,016.[1]

In 1875 an act was passed by the Congress requiring payment of the greenbacks in coin after January 1, 1879. This legislation is famous in the financial history of the country as the Resumption act.[2] Under the currency policy of the government, first formulated without authority of law by Secretary Sherman in carrying into effect the provisions of the Resumption act, and later declared by statute, that gold and

---

[1] *Report*, p. xv.

[2] See Upton's *Money in Politics*, ch. xvii. "Resumption"; and "The Future of Resumption" in *North American Review*, August, 1879.

silver shall be maintained on a parity with each other, payment of the greenbacks in "coin" was, and has been continuously since construed by the Treasury authori- ties to mean in gold; and they are so redeemed at the Treasury in Washington, and at the sub-treasuries in New York and San Francisco, on presentation and demand.

By the act of April 12, 1866, the Secre- tary of the Treasury was permitted to retire greenbacks to the amount of $10,- 000,000 during the six months ending October 12, 1866, and $4,000,000 per month thereafter. The volume of green- backs stood on June 30, 1866, very nearly at the figure of $400,000,000, and it was during these nineteen months that Secre- tary McCulloch made his reduction of some $44,000,000, leaving the amount outstand- ing in December 31, 1867, as stated, some $356,000,000. This amount was subse- quently increased to $382,000,000. Under the operation of the act of January 14, 1875, which authorized an increase in the circulation of the National banks, the Secretary of the Treasury was required to retire greenbacks to the extent of eighty per cent. of the national bank notes thereafter issued, until the amount of the greenbacks should be $300,000,000 and no more.[1] In this manner, between the last named date and May 31, 1878, $35,318,984 of the greenbacks were redeemed and retired, leaving the outstanding amount, when the act was repealed, $346,681,016, the figure at which it has since stood and now stands.

In May, 1878, an act was passed forbidding the further retirement of the legal tender notes, as above stated, and instructing the Secretary to reissue them whenever redeemed or received into the treasury from any source whatever, and to keep them in circulation.

"Since Mr. McCulloch's policy of paying —not exchanging—legal tender notes, was abruptly broken up by Congress, we have never seen the time when a majority in both houses was firmly in favor of the retirement of legal tenders," says a writer in the *North American Review* for August,

---

[1] Knox, *United States Notes*, p. 140.

1879 ; and the statement holds as good in 1895 as it did then.[1]

The fact that the law gives authority for the indefinite reissuing of the greenbacks when redeemed, without reference to the several acts under which they originally were issued, makes it impossible to tell at this day to which of the three several statutes authorizing them they are now properly attributable in their reissued form.[2]

Being redeemable in gold and not permitted by law to be retired, the $346,000,-000 of greenbacks and the $151,000,000 of treasury legal tender notes, issued under the Sherman act of 1890, make it a matter of practical impossibility for the government for any continued period of time to maintain its gold reserve of $100,000,000 in the treasury, whenever speculators or other interested persons desire to withdraw gold ; and necessitate the repeated issuing of bonds to be sold for the replenishment of the gold reserve.

---

[1] " The Future of Resumption," *North American Review*, August, 1879, p. 192.

[2] Upton, *Money in Politics*, p. 97.

These currency conditions have been succinctly and justly criticised in the following language :

" We now have laws, which direct the redemption on presentation, of the United States legal tender notes in coin, and which clothe the Secretary of the Treasury with power to provide coin for such redemption to the extent that he can command surplus revenue, or can borrow on bonds at par, bearing interest at not more than five per cent. ; but we also have laws which direct the Secretary to reissue and keep in circulation all the notes so redeemed, and all these laws are liable to repeal or modification whenever a majority of Congress, with the President, shall determine. That such a solution of the currency problem is not a safe, satisfactory, and permanently favorable one, must be obvious to every sensible observer. It leaves the right of Congress to issue legal tender notes, if not conceded, at least undenounced ; it leaves the means of continued redemption at the discretion of the Secretary of the Treasury for the time being ; and finally it exposes the whole scheme to modification or repeal by Congress or the President."[1]

This powerful and luminous criticism of the currency system, which was penned in

[1] " The Future of Resumption," *North American Review,* August, 1879.

1879, is equally applicable to-day, when "coin" has been translated to mean "gold," when the borrowing by the government on bonds can only be done at an expense not dreamed of when resumption was being provided for; when the right of the Congress to re-issue the war-greenback has been since determined by the Supreme Court, and its power to create and circulate new legal tenders is not only conceded, but has been put into practical operation by the emission from the Treasury under the Sherman act of 1890 of more than $150,000,000 of such notes, based upon silver bullion, and like the greenback, though payable at the Treasury in "gold or silver coin" at the discretion of the Secretary, practically payable in gold, and permitted by the statutes to be reissued and kept in circulation.

In February, 1879, two months after the resumption of specie payments under the act of 1875, a bill was reported to the House of Representatives, forbidding the sale of bonds for the purpose of maintaining specie payments, and directing the

Secretary of the Treasury to reissue the greenbacks, not only to the amount, but in the denominations received into the Treasury. On motion of Mr. Garfield, then a representative from Ohio, the bill was laid on the table by a vote of 141 to 110.

"The experience we are having in this House from day to day," said Mr. Garfield, on that occasion, "makes me fear that there will never be any permanent safety to business so long as there is a greenback in circulation." [1]

The legal tender quality of the greenback, which was at first repudiated and denied by the Supreme Court as unconstitutional, is now established beyond judicial question; and as bitterly as the propriety of the decision has been assailed, and its justification under any circumstances controverted, there is little doubt that the right of the Congress to give the legal tender quality to the United States Treasury issues will never again be seriously disputed in the Federal courts, so long as the present

---

[1] *Congressional Record*, February 23, 1879; Richardson *The National Banks*, page 158.

system of the absolute control of the currency by the Congress shall continue.

In spite of its legal tender feature, and the pressure of government intervention in aid of its circulation, the greenback at one time depreciated very greatly in value.[1] Since the Resumption act which made it redeemable in coin went into effect, however, in 1879, it has remained steadily at par.

It was originally provided that the forced circulation of United States legal tender notes should be ended and they should be retired by funding them in gold bonds. The writer of the luminous and prophetic article in the *North American Review* for August, 1879, already frequently quoted from in these pages, says :

" There is no doubt that the resumption clause of the act of 1875 was intended by its author, Judge Edmunds of Vermont, to provide for the permanent and absolute retirement of redeemed United States notes ; but that construction was not so clearly expressed but that Mr. Sherman, then senior senator

---

[1] General Walker, in his valuable treatise on *Money*, gives an interesting table on page 374, showing the premium on gold during the first five years of the greenback.

from Ohio, and chairman of the Finance Committee of the Senate, felt himself justified in declining to maintain it in debate. The law as passed left this point undecided, and gave to the enemies of resumption, aided by its timid or lukewarm friends, the opportunity which they afterwards seized to force upon the Treasury the law of 1878. Under this law, forming an integral part of the legislation regulating redemption, the United States notes were not to be *paid* in any ordinary acceptation of that word, since the payment of a promissory note, whether that of an individual or that of a government, involves its cancellation, and the termination of its legal existence ; they were simply made exchangeable, at par, on presentation for coin. The distinction is a vital one and cannot be too much insisted on. By the resumption law, as Judge Edmunds intended it, the notes of the government were to be paid, retired, cancelled, destroyed. They were to pass forever from the currency to be replaced by gold."

The Congress, however, repealed the provision for funding the legal tenders in gold bonds ;—a repeal which has been said by high financial authority to have been "greater than all other mistakes in the management of the war."[1]

[1] *Lalor's Cyclopædia*, article, " American Finance." Upton, *Money in Politics*, p. 89.

The ability of the government to redeem
its three hundred and forty-six millions of
greenbacks and its one hundred and fifty
millions of Sherman act Treasury notes
now in existence, depends upon three con-
tingencies. The first of these is the ability
to constantly maintain in the United States
Treasury the gold reserve, which, as has
been heretofore stated, is a surplus stock
of gold originally accumulated in anticipa-
tion of the resumption of specie payments
in 1879, and since arbitrarily fixed at one
hundred millions of dollars. Its diminution tends to decrease public confidence,
and consequently to injure business;
and it is said to be the barometer of
the national credit. Under the administration of Mr. Cleveland, the " free
gold" reserve has varied in amount from
a sum several millions in excess of that
fixed as a safe minimum to somewhere in
the vicinity of forty millions in February,
1895. Three times within twelve months
during that administration it has been
found necessary to issue government bonds
to replenish the Treasury, depleted of its

gold through the instrumentality of the legal tenders. Under our system of currency, the United States is made the prey of every gold-seeking country of the world. The Treasury itself is at the mercy of the bankers and brokers who find a profit in the exportation of gold coin and bullion; and, as illustrative of this condition, it is said that the same gold which was obtained by the Federal Treasury, under the fifty millions loan of December, 1894, in aid of the gold reserve, was withdrawn and went within a few weeks thereafter to purchase the bonds of the French municipal loan of 1895. The other two factors above alluded to, which go to make up the government's ability to redeem the legal tenders, stand in so close a relation to the existence of the gold reserve that it is difficult to segregate them as distinctive from it. They are the government's power and willingness to borrow money,—a subject already briefly alluded to; and the government's taxing power—a question of great moment and of a wide scope and meaning, beyond the contemplation of this work.

From what has been written, it is evident that the greenback is a makeshift in finance, issued originally for the purpose of paying government obligations incurred in an expensive and tremendous war, by means of a forced loan without interest from citizens of the United States.[1] It was first put into circulation by payment out of the Treasury to the soldiers and government employees, and in compensation for the munitions of war. It was essentially a war currency; and has been aptly described as "the evidence of a debt not paid, and a lien upon the future."[2] Yet its advocates have been and still are very numerous in the United States, and faith in its efficacy as a financial panacea gave rise after the Civil War to a formidable political organization known as "the Greenback party," which at one time nominated presidential and other candidates, and had a large number of adherents in certain sections of the country.[3]

[1] Upton, *Money in Politics*, ch. xiv.

[2] Lyman J. Gage's Address to the Commonwealth Club of Chicago, Oct. 27, 1894.

[3] The three planks of the Greenback party's platform were: (1) that the currency of all national and state banks and cor-

The theory of those who advocated the greenback was that it had been the means of increasing wages, of stimulating production, and of enlarging and adding to the material prosperity and comfort of the people of the whole country. Coupled with this, and of a more potential force than it will be readily credited with by the casual observer, has been the patriotic sentiment that the greenback is "stained with the blood of the Federal soldier, and helped to preserve the Union." But financiers and publicists have condemned the United States legal tender notes with great emphasis. Garfield's opinion of them has already been cited. High Democratic authority has denounced them recently, alleging that "redeemable in gold coin on demand, according to the direction of the statutes, by the Secretary of the Treasury,

---

porations should be withdrawn; (2) that the only currency should be a paper one, issued by the government; and, (3) that coin should only be paid for interest on the national debt. An interesting sketch, by Professor Alexander Johnston, of the Greenback party as originally constituted, and of its subsequent coalition with the Labor party, is given in *Lalor's Cyclopædia of Political Science*, art., "Greenback—Labor, or National Party."

10

they constitute a standing menace to the Treasury, constantly draining the gold, impairing the reserves, and necessitating the issuing of bonds to supply the necessary gold." [1]

In 1873 Prof. W. G. Sumner said of the legal tender decision of the Supreme Court in the *Legal Tender cases* that it "did as great a wrong as the Dred Scott decision, and that the latter instance shows that it is not useless to discuss a constitutional question even after the court has decided. It will not probably take a war to overthrow the principle of the Legal Tender act, but it may take a national bankruptcy." [2]

Gen. Francis A. Walker speaks of the act of 1862, creating the legal tender as "ill advised legislation," [3] and Messrs. Morrill and Collamer of Vermont, Owen Lovejoy, and Roscoe Conkling opposed it strenuously in the Congress at the time of its passage. [4]

[1] Senator David B. Hill before the Democratic Club of New York City, January 26, 1895.

[2] Sumner, *American Currency*, p. 59.

[3] Walker, *Money*, p. 374.

[4] Upton, *Money in Politics*, ch. xii ; Knox, *U. S. Notes*, pp. 129, 130 ; Walker, *Money*, p. 373.

On the contrary, John Sherman of Ohio, and Charles Sumner of Massachusetts advocated the legal tender feature of the bill,[1] and James G. Blaine said of it that " in the judgment of a large and intelligent majority of those who were contemporary with the war, and gave careful study to its progress, the Legal Tender bill was a most effective and powerful auxiliary to its prosecution."[2]

The Supreme Court of the United States, speaking of the greenbacks in 1868, said: " These notes are obligations. They bind the national faith. They are, therefore, strictly securities "; [3] and under the act of February, 1862, the court held that as " securities," they were exempt from state taxation. This effect of the Supreme Court's decision has been nullified, however, by a recent act of the Congress, making greenbacks, gold and silver certificates, Sherman treasury notes, and national bank notes subjects of state and territorial taxation as money.[4]

---

[1] Knox, *U. S. Notes*, pp. 132 and 134.
[2] *Twenty Years in Congress*, vol. i., p. 429.
[3] Bank *vs.* Supervisors, 7 Wallace, 26.
[4] Act, August 13, 1894.

By provision of statute United States notes are of such denominations not less than a dollar, as the Secretary of the Treasury may prescribe;[1] and it is made an offence, punishable by fine and imprisonment, for any person to make, issue, circulate, or pay out any note, check, memorandum, token, or other obligation for a sum less than one dollar, intended to circulate as money, or to be used in lieu of lawful money of the United States.[2]

Two peculiar forms of minor currency in frequent use during and subsequent to the war, were the "postal currency" and the "fractional currency." The first was issued under act of July 17, 1862, for the purpose of supplying small currency on the disappearance from circulation of the lesser silver coins. The demand for the postal currency was indicated by the enormous purchases of postage-stamps at the post-offices of the country, prior to its issue, and after the disappearance of the subsidiary silver.[3]

---

[1] *Rev. Stat. U. S.*, §3571.

[2] *Rev. Stat. U. S.*, §3583.

[3] Knox, *United States Notes*, p. 100.

The postal notes were superseded by the fractional paper currency issued under act of March 3, 1863, limited in amount to fifty millions of dollars, and ranging in denominations from three cents to fifty cents. This disappeared from circulation after the resumption of specie payments in 1879.[1]

In this connection it may be stated that various interest-bearing notes were issued from the Treasury at different times during the progress of the Civil War, all of which have long since disappeared from general circulation; and a discussion or description of which is unnecessary here,[2] further than to observe that of them were certain interest-bearing issues under the act of March 3, 1863, which possessed, like the greenbacks, the legal tender feature, being the only such notes ever issued by the United States Government, except the greenbacks, the "demand notes," and the Sherman Treasury notes of 1890.[3]

Among the Treasury issues of the Civil

---

[1] Knox, *United States Notes*, p. 103.

[2] Knox, *United States Notes*, ch. ix.

[3] Upton, *Money in Politics*, ch. xiii.

War period, prior to the greenbacks, were the "demand notes" authorized by the act of July 17, 1861, to the extent of $50,000,-000. They were in denominations of not less than $5, payable on demand, bore no interest, were redeemable in coin, were not originally legal tender, and were reissuable until December 31, 1862.[1] They were paid out to the government employees, and were the precursors of the greenbacks; and were subsequently made legal tenders, by act of March 17, 1862, on the advice of Secretary Chase.[2]

---

[1] Upton, *Money in Politics*, p. 69.
[2] *Id.*, ch. xiii.

IX.

As has been said, the greenback was practically a forced loan without interest, exacted by the government from its employees and creditors.[1] It was put into circulation by the purchase of gold, and by payments to government officials and clerks, and to the army and navy. But the people did not take kindly to the new currency; and though a legal tender, the banks refused to receive it and the business men to use it. A possible explanation of its unpopularity may be found in the idea which had taken possession of the public mind, that the government's revenues were inadequate to its redemption, and that the day of its payment in specie would never

---

[1] *Lalor's Cyclopædia*, article, "Refunding of Public Debt of United States."

come. As a result of the general loss of
confidence in the government's ability to
pay its Treasury issues, the greenback
rapidly depreciated in value. To relieve
this depreciation and its consequent stag-
nation and failure to circulate, and to make
a market for the government bonds which
the Treasury was forced to issue at the
time to carry on the war, the establishment
of the national banks was determined on.[1]
The waning vitality of the greenback was
reinforced by the provision of the National
Bank act that the notes of the banks
should be redeemable in the United States
Treasury legal tenders ; and the market
for the bonds was provided in the requirement that the bank circulation should be
based on government securities. Another
though lesser aim that was had in view by
the Secretary, in organizing the national
banks, was that of winning to the active
aid of the government, in its tremendous
struggle, the moneyed men and financial
leaders of the country by identifying the

---

[1] Trenholm, *The People's Money*, p. 168 ; H. W. Richardson, *The National Banks*, p. 102.

banking system actively and closely with
the government.[1]

While it is doubtless true that its primary and most desired object was the
floating of a great war debt, it is none the
less probable that the Congress in adopting
the national bank system, had at the same
time in ultimate contemplation the retirement of the greenbacks and their substitu-
tion by the notes of the banks ; for it is a
noticeable fact, that the title to the act
creating the system of banks was " an act
to provide a national currency," and that
the text of the act itself looked to the return to specie payments and the making of
coin the sole legal tender.[2] The bill creating the greenbacks, as originally reported,
expressly affirmed that they were to be
issued "for temporary purposes";[3] and
both Mr. Fessenden and Mr. Sherman,
while it was on its passage, spoke of it as
" a temporary expedient." [4]

The plan of issuing the greenback legal-

---

[1] Sherwood, *History and Theory of Money*, p. 142.
[2] Dunbar, *Theory and History of Banking*, p. 135.
[3] *Congressional Globe*, January 28, 1862, p. 522.
[4] Richardson, *The National Banks*, p. 137.

tender Treasury note had been adopted, and suggested to the Congress by Mr. Chase, at the same time with a plan of providing the "national currency" to be issued by the banks and secured by the pledge of United States bonds. Mr. Chase had hoped that the Congress would prefer the bank scheme; the Congress had adopted the Treasury-note plan; and the Secretary's desire to devise ways and means of meeting the government's urgent need of money had impelled him to approve of the greenback act even in its legal-tender feature.

In the June prior to the passage of the National Bank act, greenbacks had depreciated twenty-five per cent.; and in the month of its passage gold was at a premium of fifty. The effect of the legal-tender act of 1862 had been to destroy the government's credit abroad. No sales of bonds could be made in England during the war; and it was absolutely necessary for the government to borrow money from some source.[1]

---

[1] Sumner, *American Currency*, p. 204.

In order, therefore, to float an additional loan of the 5-20 bonds, authorized by the act of February 12, 1862, the Secretary again pushed to the front his national bank scheme that had been discarded by the Congress for the legal-tender act at the time of its former suggestion. A bill embodying his ideas was introduced in the Senate by John Sherman, of Ohio, and became a law on February 25, 1863.[1] It is an interesting and singular fact in connection with the passage of the National Bank act that the records of the debate show that Mr. Sherman, the patron of the bill, made the only speech that was made in the Senate in its favor; and that its final passage was secured only by the personal appeals of the Secretary of the Treasury, supplemented by a special message from President Lincoln.[2]

Among other provisions of the bill, in order to facilitate the negotiation of the bonds, the requirement in the act of Feb-

---

[1] Richardson, *The National Banks*, p. 47.

[2] *Appleton's Cyclopedia of American Biography*, Article, "John Sherman"; Richardson, *The National Banks*, p. 47.

ruary 12, 1862, that they should be sold
at par, was repealed; and the greenbacks
were made convertible into government
bonds at the will of the holder.

This was the original Bank Act, which
did not go into practical operation to the
extent of materially increasing the circulation until some two or three years later.
Under it only one hundred and thirty-four
banks were organized in the nine months
following its passage, and less than four
hundred and fifteen in the sixteen months
thereafter.[1]

The bank act of 1863 was not all that
could be desired in its arrangement; and
there were obscurities and possible incon- ·
sistencies which were calculated to mar its
harmonious operation. The Comptroller
of the Currency, Mr. Hugh McCulloch,
gave it careful and thorough study, and
bringing to its consideration the knowledge
of an experienced and practical banker,
recommended many necessary and substantial changes. These the Congress, in the
main, adopted in the act of June 3, 1864,

---

[1] Dunbar, *Theory and History of Banking*, p. 134.

which is practically the bank law as it now stands.[1]

The state banks were still in existence, with a large volume of currency in circulation. In January, 1861, the paper currency of the United States was furnished by sixteen hundred private corporations organized under the laws of thirty-four different states. About $150,000,000 of these state bank notes were in existence in the states which remained in the Union subsequent to April, 1861; and about $50,000,000 in the states forming the Southern Confederacy.[2] This state bank-note circulation continued all through the years of the Civil War. In order to destroy it, and thus make room for the notes of the new national banks, a ten per cent. tax on state bank issues was incorporated by the Congress in the internal revenue tax bill of 1865.[3] On June 30, 1864, the Congress had inaugurated, for the first time, the policy of taxing state bank circulation in imposing a tax of

[1] Richardson, *The National Banks*, p. 63.

[2] Richardson, *The National Banks*, ch. ii.

[3] Act, March 3, 1865 ; Act, July 13, 1866.

one per cent.   The imposition of this one per cent. tax was not designed as a revenue measure.   It was tentative, and directed towards finding out the condition of the state banks' issues, with a view to ultimately destroying their circulation by increasing the tax to a prohibitive extent. Secretary Chase said of it:

" It cannot be doubted that the object of this provision was to inform the proper authorities of the exact amount of paper money in circulation with a view to its regulation by law." [1]

It is worthy of mention, as indicative of the uncertainty of the legislative mind as to the right of imposing the ten per cent. tax, that the provision incorporating it in the internal revenue bill of 1865 was carried in the House of Representatives only by the casting vote of Speaker Colfax, and in the Senate by the close majority of two. Its constitutionality has been repeatedly denied by high authority; but the Supreme Court of the United States has taken the

---

[1] Speech of Hon. Jno. W. Daniel in United States Senate, July 21, 1892.   Veazie Bank *vs.* Fenno, 8 Wallace, 533.

legislative view, and affirmed its validity.[1] Numerous bills, however, have at various times been introduced in the Congress to repeal it, as many as nine such bills having been offered as far back as the Forty-fifth Congress; and many since.[2] Secretary Carlisle, in his scheme for the re-adjustment of the currency, as set out in his report of December, 1894, recommended its conditional repeal; and there is a strong feeling existing in the public mind in behalf of the revival of state bank issues, either under Federal restrictions, or unqualifiedly.[3]

The ten per cent. tax was laid on the advice of Secretary of the Treasury Fessenden, who had succeeded Mr. Chase in the financial administration of the government. He saw that in competition with the state banks the organization of the national banks would be infrequent and of comparatively small moment, and the bonds of the government without the local purchasers from this expected source; because,

---

[1] Veazie Bank *vs.* Fenno, 8 Wallace, 533.

[2] Richardson, *The National Banks*; p. 153.

[3] Speech of Hon. Jno. W. Daniel in United States Senate, July 21, 1892.

as a rule, the state banks could issue circulating notes without the necessity of investing any part of their capital in securities as a basis thereof, while the national banks must make a necessarily large outlay for government bonds in order to be able to issue notes. The result of the tax was that which the Secretary anticipated and desired. It was prohibitive in its effect; the state bank notes vanished from circulation; the national banks sprung into flourishing existence throughout the Union, and begun to issue note circulation; and the control of the currency was for the first time in the history of the country, and thenceforward till the present, absolutely with the Congress.[1]

The original Bank Act, revised and amended by the act of June 3, 1864, was an adaptation, with modifications in details, of several state bank systems then existing. The New York system, devised by the Rev. Dr. McVickar, Professor of Political Economy in Columbia College, New York, first established in 1838, and in successful operation thereafter continuously up to

---

[1] Dunbar, *Theory and History of Banking*, p. 133.

1861, furnished the example of currency secured on public funds, as well as the personal liability feature of directors and stockholders.[1] The "Suffolk System," prevalent in New England, furnished the scheme of redemption of issues at financial centres; and other and different systems were consulted and adapted in minor details.[2]

Under the Bank Act, the national banks were, as state banks had been, liable to local taxation. By recent legislation, not only the banks themselves, but their circulating notes, as well, are now liable to such taxation; as are the greenbacks, the gold and silver certificates, and the Sherman act Treasury notes of 1890.[3]

As stated on its face, every national bank note is secured by bonds of the government deposited with the United States Treasurer at Washington. The certificate of this fact is evidenced by the signatures

---

[1] *Lalor's Cyclopædia*, article, "American Finance." For an able and exhaustive exposition of the principles of the New York State Banking Law, see the *Democratic Review* for May, 1839.

[2] Richardson, *The National Banks*, pp. 81 and 82.

[3] Act, Aug. 13, 1894.

11

of the Treasurer and of the Register of the Treasury on the note; although the note purports to be that of the local bank issuing it, whose president or vice-president and cashier also sign it. The note is by law made receivable in all parts of the United States in payment of all taxes, excises, and all other dues to the United States except duties on imports; and also for salaries and other debts and demands owing by the United States to individuals, corporations, and associations within the United States, except interest on the public debt.[1]

The national bank notes are not unlimited legal tender; but are such only as between the banks themselves.[2] The notes are issued by the Federal government to the bank which puts them in circulation, only after the bank has deposited with the Treasurer of the United States registered bonds of the government, exceeding in value the notes to be issued. The bonds are held at the Treasury as security for the ultimate

---

[1] *Rev. Statutes U. S.*, § 5182.
[2] *Rev. Statutes U. S.*, § 5196.

redemption of the notes, none of which are ever redeemed directly from the holder by the bank itself; so that, in effect, their payment being guaranteed by the United States,[1] the notes are practically as much a national government currency as are the greenbacks, the Sherman Treasury notes, or the silver and gold certificates. They afford the only example of currency of their peculiar character in the world, full and absolute government security for bank notes existing nowhere else among the commercial nations of the earth; though the Bank of England notes have some points of resemblance in this respect to them.[2]

The bank, when furnished with these notes, issues them in turn to its customers in the usual and ordinary course of business, guaranteeing their payment, and undertaking, if called on to do so, to furnish greenbacks for any part of the issue. This singular provision of the law, incorporated in the statute, as before explained, in order

---

[1] Richardson *The National Banks*, p. 74.

[2] Dunbar, *Theory and History of Banking*, ch. x ; Walter Bagehot, *Lombard Street* (Scribners, 1892), p. 23

to revive the drooping credit of the greenback, has been commented upon by a distinguished financier and publicist, himself
once Comptroller of the Currency, as
follows:

"It is owing to the very success of these banks
that the public has come to accept it as a safe principle that all their paper money should issue from
Washington, and that they should look to Washington alone for its redemption. The application of
that mistaken deduction from the national banking
system led to the issue of coin notes. People natu-
rally thought that if the government could be
trusted to hold its own bonds as security for national
bank notes, it might be trusted to hold silver dollars
against certificates.[1]

"The national banks have been unwittingly, un-
consciously, and in my judgment, unfortunately,
educating the people and preparing the public mind
for the very thing that is now threatening them.
The moment the public began to get tired of the
weight and inconvenience of carrying about these
silver dollars, it was easy enough to suggest: 'We
will keep the dollars in Washington, and we will
issue paper certificates against them.' The public
was pleased, the inconvenience passed away, we soon
began to think that one paper dollar was as good as
another. We did not calculate that the national

---

[1] Act, Feb. 28, 1878.

bank note was the best piece of paper circulating in the country ; that next to that came the silver certificate ; and last of all the greenback. The law had inverted the order ; the law had said national bank notes must be redeemed in greenbacks ; the law had educated the people into the idea that the greenback was a better piece of paper than the national bank note, whereas the national bank note is the best piece of paper in circulation." [1]

The currency value of the national bank notes is in no respect dependent on the continued solvency of the individual national banks issuing them ; for, should the bank fail, they are made good by the government out of the bonds deposited to secure their redemption with the Treasurer at Washington.[2] They are thus rendered absolutely secure, so far as the credit of the national government can secure them ; and the greatest defect attributed to them by financiers, resulting from the character of their security, is their lack of elasticity as a so-called bank currency.

---

[1] Address of Hon. W. L. Trenholm before the University Extension Society at Philadelphia, February 10, 1892 ; published in Sherwood's *History and Theory of Money*, pages 17 and 18.

[2] *Rev. Stats. U. S.*, § 5159.

Another serious objection to them is that being national in character, and bought by the banking institution which puts them into circulation, they are by nature a commodity for which at times there is no local demand, and are therefore a matter of some expense to the bank to maintain. This being the case, the tendency of such currency is towards the commercial centres, where the demand is usually greater, for purposes of speculation, if for none other.

All national bank notes, as has been said, are required to be received in payment by all other national banks; and can be paid to the government, or used in payment by it, in all cases where specie is not required by law to be used; but the notes are not, and have never been, a legal tender between individuals.

A redemption fund of five per cent. on its circulation is, by act of June, 1874, required to be deposited by each bank with the Treasurer of the United States at Washington. By the law of 1864 provision was made for the redemption of the national bank notes at agencies in larger cities. This provision was subsequently repealed, and the Treasurer of the United States is now by law constituted the exclu- sive custodian of the five per cent. redemp- tion fund, as well as of the bonds on which the note circulation is based.[1]

By the acts of 1863 and 1864 a limitation was imposed upon the amount of bank cir- culation, the aggregate of which was fixed at $300,000,000. Later, this sum was in- creased to $354,000,000 ;[2] and finally, by the Resumption act of 1875 all restrictions as to the amount of national bank issues were abolished. At the same time by the same legislation disappeared the then exist- ing provisions of law [3] for an apportion- ment of bank-note circulation among the states according to their representative population.[4]

A number of important national banks have never chosen to issue notes, confining their business to discounts and deposits,

---

[1] Act, June 20, 1874, § 3.
[2] *Rev. Stats. U. S.*, § 5177.
[3] *Rev. Stats. U. S.*, § 5178.
[4] Dunbar, *Theory and History of Banking*, pp. 141, 142.

and to the buying and selling of exchange.[1]
Under the provision of the law of 1874
permitting banks, by placing with the
Treasurer of the United States lawful
money to enable him to redeem the notes
and to surrender *pro tanto* the bonds
securing them, provided the amount of
bonds left in deposit was not less than
$50,000, to retire their circulation to not less
than $45,000, a number of the most promi-
nent banks prior to 1878 reduced their
circulation to the minimum. This with-
drawal of notes by the banks continued
until 1878. After the resumption of specie
payment in 1879 the bank circulation increased; but it has never since reached the
amount outstanding prior to 1874.[2] Since
the resumption of specie payment the
highest point attained was at the close of
1881, when the outstanding bank notes
aggregated $325,000,000. From that time
they declined rapidly in amount, until in
October, 1890, they stood at about $125,-
000,000. This decline was doubtless due

---

[1] *Report of the Comptroller of the Currency*, 1889, p. 33.
[2] Dunbar, *Theory and History of Banking*, pp. 151, 152.

to the rapid payment, during that period of the national debt, and the large premium commanded in the market by the government bonds, which made it more profitable to the banks to withdraw their circulation and sell their bonds. Since 1890 there has been a net increase of the bank circulation from $125,000,000 to about $207,-000,000 in 1894.[1] The average annual circulation of the national banks in the United States from 1864 to 1894 was $282,801,252.[2]

A peculiar and interesting class of national bank notes was authorized in 1870 by the Congress, in the act establishing what were known as " gold banks," under the National Bank act. A number of banks on the Pacific slope, desiring to provide for the redemption of their notes exclusively in gold, were authorized to organize and to issue notes so redeemable. These notes were secured by deposit with the Treasurer of the United States of government bonds, bearing interest, payable in

---

[1] *Report of the Secretary of the Treasury*, 1894, p. xv.
[2] *Report of the Comptroller of the Currency*, 1894, p. 33.

gold. They were not to exceed eighty per
cent. of the bonds.[1] This kind of bank
was created on the theory existing in 1870
that the resumption of specie payments by
the government, in view of the losses of the
Civil War and the tremendous war debt,
was far in the then indefinite future. After
the Resumption act went into effect, the
distinction between the gold banks and the
other national banks ceased to be of importance; and provision was made in the
act of 1880 for their conversion into national banks of the ordinary kind.[2] By the
official report of 1876 there were nine of
these gold banks in existence, all located in
California, with an aggregate capital of
$4,450,000, and a note circulation of
$2,090,500.[3] The act authorizing the gold
banks limited the amount of their circulation.[4] This limit of circulation was, however, repealed by the act of January 19,
1875.[5]

[1] *Revised Statutes U. S.*, § 5185.
[2] *Supplement to Revised Statutes U. S.*, p. 278.
[3] Walker, *Money*, p. 509.
[4] *Revised Statutes U. S.*, § 5185.
[5] *Supplement to Revised Statutes U. S.*, p. 59.

In concluding this chapter on the national bank notes it may be stated, that · while the lowest denominations of the greenback, the silver certificate, and the Treasury note of 1890 is one dollar, the law provides that no bank-note shall be issued for a less sum than five dollars.[1] This, however, has only been the case since the resumption of specie payments. Prior thereto the denominations of bank-notes, as provided by statute, were one dollar, two dollars, three dollars, five dollars, ten dollars, twenty dollars, fifty dollars, one hundred dollars, five hundred dollars, and one thousand dollars;[2] but not more than one-sixth part of the notes furnished by the Treasury Department to any bank could be of a less denomination than five dollars.[3]

Repeated efforts have been made at various times to have the Congress repeal the National Bank act, and retire the notes;[4] the banks being an especial object

---

[1] *Revised Statutes U. S.*, § 5175.

[2] *Revised Statutes U. S.*, § 5172.

[3] *Revised Statutes U. S.*, § 5175.

[4] Richardson, *The National Banks*, pp. 154, 155.

of hostility to the ultra believers in the greenback.   The greatest danger which has ever threatened them, however, is the probable payment at a comparatively early date of the major part of the bonded debt of the United States on which their circulation is based.

X.

GOLD CERTIFICATES, SILVER CERTIFICATES, TREASURY NOTES OF 1890, AND CURRENCY CERTIFICATES.

GOLD certificates were first authorized by the act of March 3, 1863. The Treasurer and sub-treasurers of the United States were empowered to issue them upon deposits of gold coin and bullion in sums not less than $20. The denominations of the gold certificates were required to correspond with the denominations of the United States notes, as the ".greenbacks" are called in the statute; and the coin and bullion deposited in the Treasury, to be kept there for the purpose of redeeming them on presentation. They are used in payment of interest on the public debt and of customs duties; and the act of 1863 provided that their amount should not at any time be more than twenty per cent. in excess of the coin and bullion in the Treasury.[1]   Many of these gold certificates were issued for clearing-house purposes in denominations of $1000, $5000, and $10,000, and were so used after the passage of the National Bank act.[2]   Their issue under the act of 1863 continued until December 1, 1878, when it ceased.   They were again authorized by the act of July 12, 1882; and have since been issued and used in settling balances at the clearing houses, and for other purposes.   Under the last-named act they are issued on deposits of gold coin solely, in denominations of not less than twenty dollars, and not on deposits of coin and bullion as under the act of 1863; and correspond in their denominations with the United States notes.

When the one hundred million dollar gold reserve in the Treasury falls below that figure, the further issuing of the gold certificates is required by statute to cease, until the reserve again becomes one hundred millions in amount, when they may again be issued.   The coin deposited for

---

[1] *Rev. Statutes U. S.*, § 254
[2] Knox, *U. S. Notes.*, p. 115.

the certificates is kept for their redemption when presented.[1]

The above provision for the cessation of issue when the gold reserve drops below one hundred millions is the sole recognition in the currency statutes of the existence of such a reserve.

The gold certificates are not legal tender. They are receivable by the clearing-houses in the settlement of balances, the act authorizing them providing that no national banking association shall be a member of any clearing-house in which such certificates shall not be so receivable. They may be counted as part of the lawful reserves of the national banks, and as a matter of fact are thus largely used. This is especially the case of late years, when the disposition of the national banks has been to hoard gold, which they can easily do by means of the gold certificates without filling their vaults with the metal, the Treasury acting as its custodian for them.

The gold certificates are receivable for customs, taxes, and all public dues, and

[1] Act, July 12, 1882, § 12.

when so received may be, and under the Treasury practice are, re-issued.

The account of gold certificates outstanding November 1, 1894, was $64,308,349, a decrease of more than fourteen and a half millions in the twelve months preceding.[1]

A distinguished American writer on finance says of the gold certificates :

"They form the ideal circulating medium, a money combining the convenience of paper with the security and stability of coin."[2]

But it has been recently urged on the floor of the Congress against the gold certificates, that the United States is the only country in the world which keeps gold locked up in its Treasury, restrained from the ordinary channels of trade, and subject only to the draft of these certificates of deposit.[3]

Under the act of February 28, 1878, re-establishing the legal-tender standard silver dollar, known as the Bland-Allison act,

---

[1] *Report of the Secretary of the Treasury,* 1894, p. xv.

[2] F. A. Walker, *Money,* p. 509.

[3] Mr. Coombs of New York, in the House of Representatives, January 25, 1895.

which continued operative until the passage of the Sherman act of 1890, the holder
of such silver dollars was authorized to
deposit them with the Treasurer and sub-
treasurers of the United States in sums not
less than ten dollars, and receive therefor
silver certificates of not less than ten dollars each, corresponding in denomination
with the United States notes. The coin
so deposited, or representing these certificates, was required to be retained in the
Treasury for their redemption.

The silver certificate is not a legal tender;
but is receivable for customs, taxes, and all
public dues, and when so received, may be
reissued. It may by law be included in
the bank reserves, and used in settlement
of clearing-house balances, as is the gold
certificate.

Whatever degree of popularity the silver
certificate may have attained among "the
plain people" as a convenient representa-
tion of the bulky silver dollars, the banks
of the country have not regarded it with
favor; and in 1882 the Congress was compelled by the attitude of the banks towards

12

this peculiar kind of paper currency, to enact legislation prohibiting national banks from belonging to any clearing-house association in which silver certificates are not receivable in settlement of balances. " But," says Mr. Upton, in his volume on *Money in Politics,* " no bank has paid any attention to the act."[1]

Up to the passage of the act of August 4, 1886, the lowest denomination of silver certificates was ten dollars. By the last-named act it is provided that silver certificates shall be issued in denominations of one, two, and five dollars, and that the larger denominations may be, on presentation at the Treasury, exchanged for certificates of these smaller denominations.

" At the time of the passage of the act last referred to, permitting the issue of silver certificates in denominations of one, two, and five dollars, standard silver dollars not represented by certificates had accumulated in the treasury to the amount of $93,-959,880, although the total coinage up to that date was only $235,643,286. Within four months after that date, although in the meantime the coinage was progressing at the usual rate, the amount of free

---

[1] Page 225.

silver held in the Treasury was reduced to $71,259,-568, and it continued to decrease on account of the demand for small certificates until it became so reduced that further issues of certificates had to be limited, practically, to the current coinage of the dollars." [1]

The popular belief is that the silver certificates, like the greenbacks and the 1890 Sherman Treasury notes, or "coin notes" as they are often called, are as a matter of fact, redeemed on presentation at the Treasury directly in gold. This, however, is not true. The United States Treasury, under the existing legislation of the Congress, is not only a bank of issue, but a bank of deposit as well, and the deposits may be general or special.[2] The silver certificate represents a deposit of silver dollars, and is redeemed when so presented, with the coined silver standard dollars, whose deposit with the Treasurer is certified on its face, or is exchanged for other silver certificates of different denominations.[3] Under the statutory financial policy

---

[1] *Report of the Secretary of the Treasury*, 1894, p. lxiii.

[2] Richardson, *The National Banks*, p. 167.

[3] Act, Feb. 28, 1878, § 3. See *Treasury Circular*, § 11, cited in *Kinley's Independent Treasury*, p. 298.

of the government, nevertheless, the silver dollars so obtained in exchange for the certificates at the Treasury, may be used to purchase legal tenders, which being payable in "coin" are paid, as a matter of practice by the Treasury officials, in gold. Thus, in this roundabout method, gold is obtainable at the Treasury for the silver certificates, as it is really obtainable for all the government currency, but not directly; and the silver certificates circulate " at a gold valuation." .

On November 1, 1894, there were in existence $337,712,504 of silver certificates, over $331,000,000 of which were in circulation outside of the Treasury, showing that that amount of coined silver dollars was stored in the government vaults for their redemption.[1] The circulation of the certificates instead of the coin is due, in large measure, to the operation of the financial principle that " paper issues displace coin of equivalent denominations."[2]

This statute, which has been regarded

---

[1] *Report of the Secretary of the Treasury*, 1894, p. xv.
[2] Sumner, *American Currency*, p. 115.

by the gold standard financiers as a very
dangerous one, and which was vetoed by
President Hayes, becoming a law in spite
of his opposition by passage over his veto,
would doubtless have been repealed or
radically amended sooner than it was but
for the convenience arising from the handling of the paper substitute for the silver
dollars, which are heavy and inconvenient
for transportation.[1]

Eminent monometallic financiers have
concurred in the opinion of the danger of
the silver certificates. Mr. Lyman J. Gage
said of them, in his address delivered October 27, 1894, before the Commonwealth
Club of the city of Chicago :

"In them a dangerous volume of inferior money
has found an abnormal use. They are the most
perplexing feature in the much-involved problem
of our national finances."

Hon. John Jay Knox has said of them :

"In the opinion of those who believe in a single
gold standard, the silver certificate is a most dangerous substitute for money."[2]

[1] Knox, *U. S. Notes*, p. 153.
[2] *United States Notes*, p. 154.

There is little doubt that the Bland-Allison act was experimental no less than compromise legislation, intended to expand and increase the volume of currency, and to appease in some degree at least the clamor of the "greenbackers." For the time being it resulted in practically killing "greenbackism"; but excited in its stead a renewed demand for the free and unlimited coinage of silver by the mints of the United States at the ratio of 16 to 1.

This demand for free coinage was in a measure satisfied temporarily by the passage of the compromise act of 1890, known as the Sherman act, which added yet another new and troublesome kind of government paper currency to those already existing. In March of that year a bill was reported to the House from the Committee on Coinage, Weights and Measures, based on a plan suggested by Secretary Windom, that owners of silver bullion, not foreign, could bring it to any government mint, and obtain legal tender therefor equal to the market value of the silver redeemable on demand either in gold or silver bullion

at its then value at the government's option, or in silver dollars at the holder's
option. This bill passed the House of
Representatives, and went through the Senate with a provision added for the free and
unlimited coinage of silver; but the conference committee of the two houses struck
out the free-coinage feature; and with certain changes it became the law known as
the Sherman act on July 14, 1890.[1]

It is indicative of the shifting and uncertain temper of the Congress in matters of
financial legislation that the Senate in 1890
incorporated into the bill suggested by
Secretary Windom the free-coinage provision which was subsequently eliminated in
conference, whereas the same body in legis-
lating on the Bland-Allison act of 1878
had stricken out of the latter the House
provision for free coinage.

The Sherman act Treasury notes, or
Treasury coin notes, as they are frequently
called, were put into circulation through
the purchase of silver bullion by the United
States Treasury at the market rates, the

[1] Ehrich, *The Question of Silver*, p. 23.

notes being given in payment therefor. The bullion so purchased is not required by the act to be coined, save only in so far as may be necessary for the redemption of the notes on presentation; and in this connection provision is made in the act that "the gain or seigniorage" from such coinage is to be accounted for and paid into the Treasury.

The denominations of the Sherman Treasury notes range from $1 up to $1000. They are specifically redeemable "in gold or silver coin" at the discretion of the Secretary of the Treasury; but the statute of 1890 recites in terms that it is "the established policy of the United States to maintain the two metals on a parity with each other upon the present legal ratio, or such ratio as may be provided by law;" and in order to maintain this parity the Sherman notes are redeemed at the Treasury in gold coin. They are reissued on redemption, the act providing that when the notes are received in the Treasury they may be, which is interpreted must be, reissued.

The policy of reissuing all government

notes and certificates is pursued by the officials of the Treasury with a view to prevent too great a contraction of the currency; though to the uninterrupted execution of this policy there has been recent exception. From the date of the first issue of the Sherman Treasury notes to March 4, 1893, no silver had been paid out of the Treasury for their redemption, and none of the notes had been retired and cancelled. But between the last-named date and September 1, 1894, Secretary Carlisle paid out for the redemption of Sherman Treasury notes nearly four million standard silver dollars, coined for the purpose from the bullion purchased under the provision of the act, and retired and cancelled the notes so redeemed.[1]

There were $151,140,568 of these Treasury notes in existence November 1, 1894.[2] They are unlimited legal tender, like the Federal gold coins, the standard silver dollars and the greenbacks; differing from the

---

[1] Secretary John G. Carlisle's letter to Hon. John T. Heard in the newspapers of September 14, 1894.

[2] *Report of the Secretary of the Treasury*, 1894, p. xv.

greenbacks in that they are primarily based on silver bullion, whereas the latter were primarily based on government credit alone. They are receivable for customs duties, differing also in this respect from the greenbacks; for taxes, and for all public dues; are lawful reserves of the national banks, and are, like the greenbacks, a constant menace to the continued maintenance of the one hundred million dollar gold reserve in the United States Treasury. The "purchasing clause" of the Sherman act was repealed November 1, 1893, in extra session of the Congress called by the President for the purpose, but only after a protracted and earnest opposition on the part of the advocates in the Senate of the free and unlimited coinage of silver. This opposition was founded not so much upon the idea of approval of the Sherman act, for men of many shades of financial opinion concurred in condemning the statute, but on the idea that its repeal should be accompanied with some recognition of silver. The recognition finally achieved was but an empty show, in the incorporation into the repeal act of the declaration that it is "the policy of the United States to continue the use of both gold and silver as standard money, and to coin both gold and silver into money of equal intrinsic and exchangeable value, such equality to be secured through international agreement or by such safeguards of legislation as will insure the maintenance of the parity in value of the coins of the two metals, and the equal power of every dollar at all times in the markets and in payment of debts;" and of the further declaration in the act "that the efforts of the government should be steadily directed to the establishment of such a safe system of bimetallism as will maintain at all times the equal power of every dollar coined or issued by the United States in the markets and in the payment of debts."[1]

The currency certificates, issued under the act of June 8, 1872, have been mentioned in the previous chapter on the Clearing-House associations. While in reality currency of the country, they are properly used only for the specific purposes

[1] Act of November 1, 1893.

of settling clearing-house balances, and of furnishing a part of the legal reserves of the banks. On November 1, 1894, there were in existence of such currency certificates $54,325,000,[1] as against $22,425,000 on the corresponding date in 1893, an increase of $31,900,000 due to the necessities of the clearing-houses during and immediately subsequent to the panic of 1893.

The currency certificates are issued on the deposit of greenbacks, which are required to be held as special deposits in the Treasury and used only for the redemption of the currency certificates, which are also known as "certificates of deposit."[2]

In the recent raids upon the gold reserve of the Treasury these currency certificates have been found convenient by the banks holding them for use in withdrawing gold. Their denominations being large, and possessing practically the equivalence of the greenbacks deposited to redeem them, the production of a comparatively small number of the certificates at the Treasury for

---

[1] *Report of the Secretary of the Treasury*, 1894, p. xv.
[2] *Revised Statutes United States*, § 5194.

redemption results in a proportionately large diminution of the gold reserve.

Mr. J. K. Upton, a distinguished former assistant secretary of the Treasury, says that, under the authority of the act creating the currency certificates, " banks employ the public treasury to keep them in notes, the denominations of which may suit their convenience ; turning into the Sub-Treasury one day worn notes of undesirable denominations, obtaining certificates therefor to be redeemed the next day in new notes of desired denominations, compelling the Sub-Treasury officers to make the exchange at Washington at the expense of the government. No other advantage in the plan has yet become evident." [1]

---

[1] Upton, *Money in Politics*, p. 262.

XI.

THE theory that the Federal Government possesses the exclusive power of both creating and regulating the currency of the country, a theory that was the outgrowth of the alleged implied powers of the Constitution, according to the Federalist doctrine, was first suggested by Alexander Hamilton in his great *Report on a National Bank.*[1]

The question of the right of the general government to create and maintain a national bank was brought before the Supreme Court of the United States in the case of *McCulloch vs. Maryland,*[2] which grew out of legislation by the State of Maryland imposing a tax upon banks not chartered

---

[1] *Reports on the Finances*, vol. i., p. 54.
[2] 4 Wheat., 316.

by the legislature of that state. Chief-Justice Marshall delivered the unanimous opinion of the court, presenting in the most logical and powerful manner the Federalist view, as propounded by Hamilton in his *Report;* and holding that there was no power in the state to impose a tax upon national bank issues, and that such a tax was therefore void, as repugnant to the Constitution. The case of *McCulloch vs. Maryland* was decided in 1819. In 1824, in the case of *Osborne vs. The Bank of the United States,*[1] the Supreme Court reaffirmed the principle established in *McCulloch vs. Maryland,* that the states had no right to tax the Bank of the United States; and Mr. Justice Johnson, in delivering a dissenting opinion on the ground of want of Federal jurisdiction, propounded for the first time from the bench of that court the principle of exclusive control by the central government over the currency,[2] asserting that the Federal authority to in-

---

[1] 9 Wheat., 738.
[2] Dabney, " Paper Money," *Va. State Bar Association Reports*, vol. vii., p. 194.

corporate a bank tended "to restore that power over the currency which the framers of the Constitution evidently intended to give to Congress alone."[1]

While recent congressional legislation has established the right of the states to tax all paper currency created by the government, in the provision that "circulating notes of national banking associations and United States legal-tender notes and other notes and certificates of the United States payable on demand, and circulating or intended to circulate as currency, and gold, silver, or other coin shall be subject to taxation as money on hand or deposit under the laws of any state or territory, provided that any such taxation shall be exercised in the same manner and at the same rate that any such state or territory shall tax money, or currency circulating as money within its jurisdiction,"[2] the far-reaching principle asserted by Mr. Justice Johnson has, by *post bellum* judicial deter-

[1] 9 Wheat., 873.
[2] Act, August 13, 1894, *U. S. Statutes at Large, 53d Congress, 1894,* ch. 281, p. 278.

mination, become definitely fixed in the most recent of the legal-tender cases decided by the Supreme Court.

The first decision of importance by that tribunal with reference to the legal tenders was that of *The Bank vs. The Supervisors*,[1] which was rendered in 1868. In that case the question was presented whether the United States notes were fiat money or government obligations. Chief - Justice Chase, delivering the opinion of the Court, said :

" These notes are obligations of the United States. Their name imports obligation. Every one of them expresses upon its face an engagement of the nation to pay to the bearer a certain sum. The dollar note is an engagement to pay a dollar, and the dollar intended is the coined dollar of the United States ; a certain quantity in weight and fineness of gold or silver, authenticated as such by the stamp of the government."

The question of the power of Congress to make the United States note a legal tender for the payment of debts arose in several cases that came before the Supreme

---

[1] 7 Wallace, 26.

13

Court, but was successfully avoided by the court's decisions on other gro unds until the issue was at last and unavoidably squarely presented in the case of *Hepburn vs. Griswold.*[1] The court at its December term, 1869, by a vote of five to three, held the act creating the greenback unconstitutional in so far as it made the notes a legal tender for debts prior to the date of the act, Chief-Justice Chase delivering the opinion. The court held further that the legal-tender clause of the act was unnecessary and improper, and argued that it was the quality which the greenbacks possessed of receivability for public dues, and not their legal-tender attribute, which caused them to circulate.

Justice Grier, who had been one of the five judges constituting the majority in the case of *Hepburn vs. Griswold,* resigned in February, 1870; and in March of that year Justices Strong and Bradley took the two vacant seats upon the bench.

The act increasing the number of judges of the Supreme Court from eight to nine

---

[1] 8 Wallace, 603.

had been passed April 10, 1869, while the case of *Hepburn vs. Griswold* was before the court. Mr. H. W. Richardson in his volume on *The National Banks*, says :

" It is not disputed that these appointments were made for the purpose of over-ruling the decision of the Court in the case of *Hepburn vs. Griswold ;* for although that decision applied strictly to such contracts only as were outstanding on the 25th of February, 1862, when the legal-tender act was approved, it was seen that the entire principle of the law was involved, and it was feared that with gold still at 120, the notes, by some subsequent decision, might be deprived of their forced currency. If this had happened, the only consequence would have been that instead of reckoning gold at 120 and the notes at par, people would have quoted the notes at 83 and gold at par ; for it would have been held that outstanding contracts must be regarded as obligations to pay notes and not coin." [1]

A majority of the court as re-constituted, at the December term, 1870, four judges dissenting, ordered that counsel for the parties denying the validity of the legal-tender clause, and the Attorney General of the United States be heard upon the questions :

---

[1] *The National Banks*, pp. 127, 128.

1. Is the act of Congress known as the Legal Tender act constitutional as to contracts made before its passage?

2. Is it valid as applicable to transactions since its passage?

In what are known as *the Legal Tender cases*, the court, in May, 1871, by a majority of one, and without any change of opinion on the part of the judges who had decided *Hepburn vs. Griswold,* declared the Legal Tender act constitutional and valid as to contracts made both before and after its enactment, reversing *in toto* its former decision.[1]

Mr. Justice Strong delivered the court's opinion, prefacing the grounds of decision with the statement that *Hepburn vs. Griswold* had been " decided by a divided court, and by a court having a less number of judges than the law then in existence provided that this court shall have. These cases have been heard by a full court, and they have received our most careful consideration."

---

[1] The Legal Tender Cases, 12 Wallace, 457.

Mr. Justice Bradley read a concurring opinion, in which was outlined that extreme doctrine promulgated by the court at a later date in the case of *Juilliard vs. Greenman*, which, in making the Congress the sole judge and arbiter of the vague and undefined constitutional powers therein asserted as belonging to it, invests that body with a plenitude of legislative authority that is " practically absolute and unlimited."

In his opinion Justice Bradley, after describing the power of the Congress to give bills of credit the quality of legal tender, as an incident flowing almost as a matter of course from the power to issue such bills, proceeded significantly to say :

" I do not say that it is a war power, or that it is only to be called into exercise in time of war ; for other public exigencies may arise in the history of a nation which may make it expedient and imperative to exercise it. But of the occasions when and of the times how long it shall be exercised and in force, it is for the legislative department to judge."

In the case of *Juilliard vs. Greenman,*[1]

[1] 110 *U. S. Reports*, 421.

decided by the Supreme Court, March 3, 1884, " the single question," as stated by the court in its opinion, was, " whether notes of the United States issued in time of war, under acts of Congress declaring them to be a legal tender in payment of private debts, and afterwards in time of peace redeemed and paid in gold coin at the Treasury, and then reissued under the act of 1878, can, under the Constitution of the United States, be a legal tender in payment of such debts."

Upon a full consideration of the case, after hearing elaborate and able argument of eminent counsel,—among those denying the right of the Congress to confer upon the re-issued greenback the legal-tender quality being Senator George F. Edmunds of Vermont, the author of the Resumption act of 1875, the court had no hesitation in deciding the question propounded in the affirmative. Mr. Justice Gray delivered the opinion; the only one of the judges lifting a dissenting voice being Mr. Justice Field, who unwaveringly maintained the position that he had first assumed when the case of

Hepburn vs. Griswold decided the legal-
tender clause to be unconstitutional.
The court, premising its opinion with
the assertion that "a constitution, establishing a frame of government, declaring
fundamental principles and creating a national sovereignty, and intended to endure
for ages and to be adapted to the various
crises of human affairs, is not to be interpreted with the strictness of a private contract," proceeded to the deduction "as a
logical and necessary consequence that Congress has the power to issue the obligations
of the United States in such form, and to
impress upon them such qualities as currency for the purchase of merchandise and
the payment of debts, as accord with the
usage of sovereign governments."

This interpretation of the basic law, Mr.
Justice Field, in his dissenting opinion,
says, "fully carried out, would change
the whole nature of our Constitution and
break down the barriers which separate a
government of limited from one of unlimited powers."

Hamilton never taught, and the most

ardent Federalist of the earlier days of the Republic never claimed for the central government, such transcendent and pervasive powers as are included in the doctrine enunciated in *Juilliard vs. Greenman*, when carried to its legitimate conclusions.

The decision of the court came as a shock to many of the ablest statesmen, financiers, and political economists of the country; and although there has since been sought to be passed through the Congress provision for the amendment of the Federal Constitution expressly prohibiting such powers as this tremendously far-reaching decision of the court conceded it, the act and its interpretation still stand together in eloquent testimony that the "heavy and unsteady hand" of the Congress remains clenched upon the currency system of the country with a more relentless and unshaken grasp than ever before in all its history.[1]

In concluding this sketch of the principal cases involving a judicial construction by the Supreme Court of financial legislation by the Congress, it is only necessary

---

[1] Knox, *United States Notes*, p. 166.

to refer briefly to the case of the *Veazie Bank vs. Fenno,*[1] in which the prohibitive ten per cent. tax on state bank issues was held to be valid and constitutional.

As stated by Chief-Justice Chase, who delivered the opinion of the court, the question which presented itself for decision was :

"Whether the second clause of the 9th section of the act of Congress of the 13th of July, 1866, under which the tax in this case was levied and collected, is a valid and constitutional law."

That clause was as follows :

" Every national banking association, state bank, or state banking association, shall pay a tax of ten per centum on the amount of notes of any person, state bank or state banking association used for circulation, and paid out by them after the first day of August, 1866, and such tax shall be assessed and paid in such manner as shall be prescribed by the Commissioner of Internal Revenue."[2]

Counsel representing the bank insisted that the tax was unconstitutional, because it was not a tax imposed for the sake of

[1] 8 Wallace, 533.
[2] 14 *Stats. at Large*, 146 ; *Rev. Stats. U. S.*, § 3412.

revenue, but that its true purpose was to destroy the state banks; that if the Congress, by discriminating taxation, could destroy the state banks, it could equally, in the same manner, destroy the railroad system of the states; and that if it should be determined as it would necessarily have to be determined if the tax should be sustained, that the taxing power of the Congress was unlimited and could not be inquired into by the court, then the Congress was supreme to legislate without any limitations, provided it was done in the form of levying a tax.

The case was decided December 13, 1869, in favor of the tax, two of the judges dissenting. Chief-Justice Chase admitted in his opinion that the object of the legislative provision was undoubtedly to regulate by law the paper money in circulation; and asserted that " having in the exercise of constitutional powers undertaken to provide a currency for the whole country, it cannot be questioned that Congress may constitutionally secure the benefit of it to the people by appropriate legislation. To this end Congress has denied the quality of legal tender to foreign coins, and has provided by law against the imposition of counterfeit and base coin on the community. To the same end, Congress may restrain, by suitable enactment, the circulation as money of any notes not issued under its own authority."

Secretary Fessenden's scheme was thus firmly established and rendered successful by the Supreme Court; and the right of taxation by the Congress of "the powers and faculties of the state governments, which are essential to their sovereignty and to the efficient and independent management and administration of their internal affairs,"[1] even to the extent of thereby prohibiting and destroying such management and administration, was definitely and unequivocally determined by ultimate judicial decision.

---

[1] Justice Nelson's dissenting opinion in *Veazie Bank* vs. *Fenno.*

XII.

CONCLUSION.

In his admirable and discriminative treatise on *Congressional Government,* Mr. Woodrow Wilson observes that a "policy cannot be either prompt or straightforward when it must serve many masters. It must either equivocate or hesitate, or fail altogether. It may set out with clear purpose from Congress, but get waylaid or maimed by the Executive." [1] If we recognize the correctness of the principle enunciated as applicable to the ordinary policies of our system of government, how much more profoundly must we of necessity be impressed with its application to currency legislation and administration. Especially must this be the case, when we reflect not only upon the frequent and often inevitable

---

[1] *Tenth Edition,* p. 283.

disagreements and collisions that must oc-
cur between the legislative and executive
departments, but upon the more remarkable phenomenon apparent in the divisibil-
ity of authority in the matter of originating
the currency legislation of the Congress.
The Greenback act, for example, had its
inception in the House Committee on
Ways and Means, whose subjects of jurisdiction are defined to be revenue and such
measures as purport to raise revenue, and
the bonded debt of the United States,[1] and
not in the Committee on Banking and Currency, which is the committee charged
with the jurisdiction of bills originating
currency and banking measures, and from
which the uninitiated observer would be
readily led to look for such legislation to
emanate. When it is reflected, however,
that the primary object of the greenback
legislation was not to establish a permanent character or system of paper currency,
but to create and float a government war
debt, it is not altogether difficult to under-

---

[1] *Rules and Practice*, House of Representatives, first session, Fifty-third Congress, page 314.

stand why it should have thus originated. So when we come to consider similar legislation in 1890, by virtue of which legal-tender Treasury notes were created and issued on the security of a deposit of silver bullion, we shall not be surprised to learn for like reasons that the act had its origin either with the Committee on Ways and Means, because its effect is, no less than that of the Greenback act, to create a public debt; or with the Committee on Currency and Banking, because it unquestionably authorizes and directs the issuing by the Treasury of a circulating medium ; or finally, with the Committee on Coinage, Weights and Measures, because, as a matter of historical fact, the act was a compromise and makeshift measure, resulting from the contest between the advocates and opponents in the Congress of the free and unlimited coinage of the standard silver dollar by the government mints at the ratio of six-teen to one. The Senate Finance Committee could not, without a violent stretch of prerogative, have originated any single one of the several species of Treasury paper

money now in circulation, because there is
no one of them which does not represent a
government debt, and has, therefore, indirectly at least had its genesis in a " bill for
raising revenue," which must, by virtue of
the Federal Constitution,[1] originate in the
House of Representatives.

The vacillation and uncertainty of such
a legislative policy in regard to the currency, as are indicated in the methods described, are emphasized and made painfully
apparent by comparison with the policies
and methods of the great commercial nations of Europe.[2]

As an inevitable result of the division of
authority among the congressional committees in the matter of originating currency
bills, and of the confusion arising in the
minds of legislators themselves as to the
real character and significance of the paper
money created by the Congress, legislation
on this subject lacks sequence, is bound by

---

[1] *Constitution of the United States*, article 1, § 7.

[2] Dunbar, *Theory and History of Banking*, chs. vii, viii, ix,
x, and xi ; Walter Bagehot, *Lombard Street ;* Wilson, *Congressional Government*, Tenth Edition, ch. iii.

no fixed rules or principles, drifts helplessly with the current of temporary popular passion or ignorance, and is absolutely impossible to be foreshadowed from one session of the Congress to another. The uncertainty thereby created in the minds of the people as to what they may have to look forward to from year to year in the way of congressional enactments about money necessarily leaves its indelible impress upon the business of the country, and destroys the stability of that general confidence which is essential to the steady growth and progress of all enterprise.[1]

In arriving at a correct understanding of the peculiar methods of the national legislature in dealing with questions of the currency, over which it has since 1865 assumed absolute and unqualified control, we must inevitably be struck with the existence of a fact that is perhaps without parallel in modern governments, viz.: the lack of authority on the part of the executive department of finance in the United States

---

[1] Edward Atkinson, " Battle of Standards." *The Forum*, April, 1895.

to even suggest, much less direct legislation
on currency subjects. Of the thirty-four
reports required by statute to be made, the
most of them annually, and some oftener,
by the Secretary of the Treasury to the
Congress, with respect to matters within
his jurisdiction as the administrative financial officer of the government, the only one
which necessarily touches matters of the currency is that on "the cost of transportation
of silver coin by registered mail or otherwise."[1] It is true that the Secretary may,
and often does,[2] in his annual report on the
general subject of "finance, containing estimates of the public revenue, and public
expenditures for the fiscal year then current, and plans for improving and increasing the revenues from time to time for the
purpose of giving information to Congress
in adopting modes of raising the money
requisite to meet the public expenditures,"[3]
suggest to the Congress such changes and
reforms of the currency as may commend

---

[1] *Rules and Practice of Fifty-third Congress*, p. 605.
[2] *Report of Secretary of Treasury for 1894*, p. lv.
[3] *Revised Statutes U. S.*, § 257.

14

themselves to his favorable consideration. But his suggestions are always gratuitous, because unasked for by statute; and are, doubtless on that account, not always treated with the consideration they deserve. The language of the act under which the Secretary's chief report is made, and the absence of any provision for a specific report on the general state of the currency, only serve to emphasize the assertion that the raising of revenue is the first consideration in the congressional administration of federal finance, and to recall vividly to mind the fact more than once heretofore adverted to in these pages, that the legislation creating the current paper circulation was not primarily intended to establish a sound and permanent system of circulating medium, but had for its object the floating of a government debt by a forced circulation of paper; and that even the National Bank act, which had its inception in the need of the government to find a local market for its bonds, falls in a way within the category in which the other currency enactments are thus placed.

As the natural result of a system which does not invite the knowledge and technical skill of expert financiers, but leaves everything to the uncertain and haphazard capacity of legislators, who may or may not be ignorant of the subjects concerning which they legislate, the conditions of the congressional currency have been recently described by the chief executive officer of the Treasury department as "constituting a monetary system unlike that of any other enlightened government in the world."[1] As has been stated, the suggestions of the Secretary when made without invitation to the Congress with regard to reforms in the currency are observed to carry so little weight, and to be received by that body with such entire indifference, that Mr. Bryce is led on this account, among others, to conclude that the Congress does not look to the Treasury Secretaries "for guidance as in the early days it looked to Hamilton and Gallatin;"[2] while Mr. Woodrow Wilson declares that having "at first neither

[1] *Report of Secretary of Treasury for 1894*, p. lii.
[2] *The American Commonwealth*, vol. i., p. 175, (2d ed.).

president nor federal judiciary, the Congress now on occasion rules both with easy mastery and with a high hand."[1]

The fact that the two committees of the House on Coinage, Weights and Measures, and on Banking and Currency, and the Finance committee of the Senate, are generally constituted of members, the most of whom may be, and very frequently are, technically skilled and exceptionally well informed in the peculiar subjects that will fall within the original jurisdiction of these legislative sub-divisions, does not lessen the constantly imminent danger of inappropriate or unsound currency enactments; for, as has been shown, these committees do not control without qualification the power of originating such legislation, nor does any one of them. Nor are the bills which they may properly prepare and bring forward usually regarded as satisfactory in all respects by other members less skilled and less learned in the subject than they, who, for political or imagined economic reasons, may succeed in loading them with amend-

---

[1] *Congressional Government,* p. 53, (10th ed.).

ments which utterly destroy their original meaning. When such a bill safely runs the gauntlet of either the House or the Senate, it must then be acted on by the other body. Again it is amended, or changed or emasculated; and then the conference committee from the two houses gets possession of it, and in the majority of cases it comes back to its parent house in the shape of a compromise or makeshift, in which its originator sees not the faintest resemblance to his bill as introduced.

Out of all this irresponsibility of any single group or smaller body of men, for the character and effect of the financial measures proposed by them, as is the case in other civilized countries, have grown the complexities and dangers of a currency system that has only until recently failed to bring about confusion and calamity because of the tremendous territorial extent and wonderful material and physical resources of the United States.[1] Even with these great advantages, possessed by no other peo-

---

[1] Edward Atkinson : " Battle of Standards," *Forum*, April 1895.

ple in the world, by the aid of which the
country has managed to struggle along under the burdens of an unparalleled pension
list and of an anomalous and absurd system
of currency, it scarcely admits of doubt or
denial that foolish financial legislation has
more than once contributed to business depression, and afforded the opportunity for
speculators and schemers to plunder the
government of the people's money.[1]

A brief *résumé* of the most salient and
noteworthy characteristics and attributes
of the several kinds of currency in circulation will serve to give perspective, from
another point of view, to the picture which
has been sought to be drawn in these
chapters.

The greenback is the evidence of a debt
still due from the government unpaid to
the holder, and is " a lien upon the future."
It represents a forced loan, without interest, based upon the government's credit.
Its circulation at par with gold is maintained by the dynamics of its legal-tender

---

[1] For a history of " Black Friday " which grew out of the
greenback legislation, see *Upton's Money in Politics*, ch. xix.

feature and of the statutory declaration by
the Congress as to the government's financial policy, supplemented by the practice
of the Treasury officials, unauthorized by
law, of redeeming it on presentation with
gold. Its legal-tender quality is unlimited
in all cases of debt, and it is receivable in
payment of all dues to the government except duties on imports, and of all claims
against the government except interest on
the public debt. It differs conspicuously
from the Treasury note of 1890, which in
other respects it so greatly resembles, in its
lack of receivability for customs duties.
When the greenback is redeemed at the
Treasury it must be reissued, and it is thus
an inconvertible paper currency.

The Sherman Treasury note of 1890 is
more nearly like the greenback than any
other existing species of paper money issued by the Federal Government. It is the
evidence of a debt of the United States to
the holder, and it represents a loan without interest. It is based in part on the
credit of the government, and in part on
a mass of uncoined silver bullion stored

in the vaults of the National Treasury. Its issue against this bullion is "upon a ratio which greatly overvalues that metal as compared with the standard unit of value in this and the other principal commercial countries." [1]   Its circulation at par is maintained, like that of the greenback, by force of its legal-tender feature and of the statutory declaration of the Congress as to the government's financial policy, which is so construed in practise by the Treasury officials as that, without express direction of law, they are in the habit of redeeming the Treasury note, on presentation, with gold. Its quality of legal tender is absolute and unlimited, and it is receivable for all debts and demands of and against the government, including customs duties.

The two foregoing species of circulating medium represent the entire legal-tender paper currency in existence in the United States. As has been stated, they are in forced circulation, and their capacity to circulate rests in no small measure upon

---

[1] *Report of the Secretary of the Treasury*, 1894, p. li.

the legal-tender attribute conferred upon them by the government,—a quality of currency that does not exist in the media of international exchanges, which are made in gold and silver, by weight and fineness, without reference to any peculiar attribute that may be sought to be affixed to them by legislation.[1]

A well-informed writer says that the United States " have had paper money in every shape, and issued for every variety of purpose that the history of finance shows to be known to any country in the world. There has been inconvertible and convertible paper money, and paper nominally convertible but really inconvertible; it has been issued by the general government, by the state governments, and by corporations under government charters; it has been legal tender and not legal tender, and the proverbial ingenuity of the Connecticut mind discovered a compromise between these two; it has been based on landed security, on the security of taxes, and on

---

[1] Edward Atkinson, " Battle of Standards," *Forum*, April, 1895.

no other security than the pure credit of
authority of the government—*i. e.*, ' fiat
money '; its causes of issue have been to
meet extraordinary government expenditures; to meet current government expenditures; for the professed purpose of
affording a circulating medium, and as a
loan for the promotion of industry. Issues of fiat money have nearly all originated
in the necessities of war. The first issue
by Massachusetts in 1690 was to pay the
cost of the disastrous expedition against
Canada. Further issues were made for a
like purpose in 1709, and the other New
England colonies with New York and New
Jersey joining in the expedition, they, too,
issued fiat money to defray the expenses.
Virginia made its first issue to defray the
expenses of Braddock's expedition; South
Carolina to meet the charge of an expedition against the Spanish settlement of St.
Augustine; the continental currency was
issued to pay the charges of the Revolu-
tionary War; all the states made large
issues for the same purpose; and the greenback of to-day came into existence through

the government needing money to put down the Rebellion." [1]

It remained, however, for the Federal Congress, sitting in the tenth decade of the nineteenth century, to create an irredeemable legal-tender fiat paper currency, under the conditions of profound peace and an overflowing Treasury, for the remarkable purpose of effecting a compromise settlement between the contending advocates and opponents of the free and unlimited coinage of silver at the government's mints.

If the greenback and the Sherman Treasury note may not improperly be described as the irredeemable bank issues of a great Federal National Treasury bank, for even the temporary redemption of which a coin reserve, though unauthorized by law, must, after the approved methods of banking, be maintained at all hazards and gigantic cost, with no less impropriety or inaccuracy may the gold, silver, and currency certificates of the government be designated as certificates of

---

[1] Cuthbert Mills, "The Permanence of Political Forces," *North American Review*, January, 1880.

deposit issued by the same Federal bank,
inasmuch as they are in the nature of de-
claratory government certificates that the
National Treasury has received, and holds,
stores, and preserves ready for forthcoming
on demand, the gold coin, silver coin, and
legal-tender notes which they respectively
represent; and this, too, without advantage
to the government which gains no profit
by the use of such deposits, but entirely
for the benefit and convenience of the certificate holder, and free of cost or charge
to him. They are, in other words, evidence of a special debt, due from the
government to the holder of the certificate of each kind, payable on presentation at the Treasury in the specific character of currency which is certified to
have been deposited. While the government pays no interest on this debt it de-
rives no benefit therefrom, and acts merely
in the capacity of custodian and insurer
of the deposits. Yet, under the interpretation placed by the Treasury Department
upon the government's statutory declaration of its financial policy, the provision in

the several acts authorizing such certificates, that when redeemed they "may be reissued" is construed to be as imperative and mandatory as in the case of the greenback, which the statute says "shall be reissued" on redemption. The excuse for such an interpretation that a failure to reissue the certificates would contract the currency is untenable, because there is locked up in the Treasury a dollar of other currency for every dollar represented by such certificates. The continued existence of the certificates of deposit, used as currency, is but one of the many anomalous and unique features of the existing system of congressional currency.

Though the several kinds of currency represented by the certificates of deposit, viz., gold coin, standard silver dollars, and legal-tender paper, all possess an unqualified legal-tender capacity, none of the three kinds of certificates possesses such an attribute, either limited or unlimited. They circulate, therefore, or two of them at least may be said to circulate, viz., the silver certificate and the currency certificate, because of the legal-tender quality not in them but behind them, and of the government's financial policy, which makes them ultimately, if indirectly, all payable in gold at the Treasury.

The notes of the national banks, while constituting a character of currency superior in many respects to any of the paper money issued directly by the Treasury, are anomalous in some of their peculiarities. The plan on which they are issued was perhaps more maturely considered before adoption than was any of those on which the several species of government issues were based; and yet the national bank notes present the singular features of being convertible into an inferior kind of paper money, viz., the greenbacks; of being legal tender only between the banks; of being secured absolutely by the pledge of government bonds; of being dependent for their existence on the existence of a national interest-bearing debt; of being redeemable not at the bank of issue, but at the Treasury of the Federal government, and of being definitively limited and fixed in amount by the amount of government securities owned by the bank which issues them. Whenever the premium on the government bond exceeds the value of the profit to be derived from the circulation of the notes, it is to the interest of the bank to retire its circulation as far as possible and sell its bonds ; hence the more valuable the bonds become for purposes of private investment, the greater the tendency of the banks to withdraw their note circulation.

Thus the whole scheme of Federal paper money, if a jumble of incoherent and un-correlated acts of the Congress may be denominated a scheme, is the inconsequential, incongruous, and unscientific result of extravagant and hazardous legislative experiments.

From the standpoint of their relation to the Federal Treasury the government issues are seen on investigation to present a condition no less remarkable than that which is apparent from a comparison of the several species, one with another. The Treasury, in putting its legal-tender notes in circulation, exercises one of the functions of a national bank of issue; and in receiving deposits of gold coin, silver dollars, and legal-tender notes, and issuing certificates therefor, exercises another banking function. While possessing, however, these two very potential and conspicuous features of a bank engaged in conducting a regular and well defined banking business, it lacks entirely other necessary and characteristic powers of such a bank, the deprivation of which makes it in certain directions conspicuously feeble and insufficient. For example, though a bank of issue and deposit, it cannot lend money on the best security. Its active influence on the money market, with which it is so closely connected, in times of emergency is therefore practically slight; its passive influence reflected in the rise and fall of the gold reserve, is tremendous. Any ability to use its reserve as ordinary bank reserves are used, in financial crises, is not possessed by it. A sound political economist lays down the principle that "whatever bank or banks keep the ultimate banking reserve of the country must

lend that reserve most freely in time of
apprehension, for that is one of the characteristic uses of the bank reserve, and the
mode in which it attains one of the main
ends for which it is kept."[1]

In such exigencies, the reserve in the
Federal Treasury, instead of being used in
the manner described, is sought most vigorously to be preserved and retained ; and the
greater the general financial distress, the
more desperate are the efforts of the Treasury officials to sustain and build up the reserve by the sale of bonds. The marked
contrast between the policy governing the
Treasury in this respect and that of the
Bank of England under such circumstances,
is graphically indicated by Mr. Bagehot
in his description of the English money
market.[2]

In considering these striking characteristics of the Federal Treasury, we are again,
from another standpoint, confronted with
the proposition hereinbefore stated, that
the primary object of all Federal legisla-

[1] Bagehot, *Lombard Street*, p. 64.
[2] *Lombard Street*, ch. ii., § II. (American ed., 1892).
15

tion with reference to finance matters is the raising of revenue, and that only as secondary to that has legislation for the purpose of securing a sound and stable currency been regarded by the Congress. The limits of this chapter do not admit of the further discussion of the peculiarities, inconsistencies, and defects of the Federal money system as it exists. Beyond a recital of the uses to which the Sub-Treasury has been perverted from its original form, it is not now proposed to pursue the subject further.

Says Professor Kinley:

" In addition to its intended duties of receiving and disbursing government money, the Independent Treasury now discharges the following functions also : First, it issues notes like a bank, and it protects these notes by keeping a reserve whose ratio to the notes issued approximates that usually kept by the banks ; second, it receives deposits and issues therefor certificates, which pass from hand to hand as money, and it keeps a deposit from which to cash the checks of disbursing officers ; third, the issue of government paper necessitates the duty of redemption by the Treasury as by banks ; redemption, that is, in the sense of the exchange of one

kind of money for another, and it also acts as agent
of the national banks for the redemption of their
notes ; fourth, the Independent Treasury transfers
money for individuals from one part of the country
to another, free of charge or at less cost than can
be done, for example, by the banks ; and finally, it
has by the law of July, 1890, been charged with
what is essentially the work of a silver bullion
broker. These powers of the Independent Treasury must be borne in mind in seeking to determine
the nature and extent of its influence on the business of the country to-day." [1]

This concluding brief *resumé* of some of
the principal facts set down in the preceding pages can, of necessity, be little else
than suggestive of the more thorough and
exhaustive criticism to which the system
described is liable. If the facts presented
possess aught of significance in themselves,
they would seem to emphasize and illus-
trate beyond argument the tremendous importance of a separation of the government
from the money market ; to demand in-
sistently that "the heavy and unsteady
hand" of the Federal Congress shall be
withdrawn from its unqualified and abso-

---

[1] *The Independent Treasury of the U. S.*, p. 122.

lute control of the currency of domestic commerce and business; and to vindicate with an irrefutable logic the statesmanship and financial wisdom of those of our fathers who devised and created the Independent Treasury scheme of fifty odd years ago, which made gold and silver the sole money of the Treasury and " divorced the government from the banks." ·

INDEX.

Act, the National Bank, 56 ;
the Coinage, of 1873, 96 ;
the Bland-Allison, 106 ; the
Sherman, of 1890, 112 ; the
Greenback, of 1862, 125.
Associations of banks as clearing-houses, 68.
Attacks on the Treasury, 143,
148.

Balances, clearing-house, and
legislation, 69.
Bank of the United States,
the first, 5 ; removal of the
deposits from the, 39 ;
notes of the, 97.
Bank Act, the original National, 156 ; genesis of the
National, 160.
Bank notes, 151.
Bank, The, vs. *The Supervisors*, 193.
Bills of credit, prohibited to
the states, 6 ; issued by the
Federal government, 128.
Blaine, J. G., on the legal-
tender act, 147.
Bland-Allison act, 176 ; restored the coinage of the
standard silver dollar, 104 ;
passage of the, 106 ; silver
dollars coined under the,
110.
Board of Treasury, 24.
Bond issues, to maintain the
gold reserve, 86 ; to maintain specie payments, 138.
Bullion, purchase of silver,

under the Sherman act,
111 ; amount of silver, purchased under the Sherman
act, 113.
Bureau of Engraving and
Printing, 59.

Calhoun, John C., on Con-
gressional control of the
currency, 7 ; on the Independent Treasury act, 45.
California, discovery of gold
in, 103 ; and the " gold
banks," 169.
Certificates, issued by the
Treasury, 52 ; clearing-
house gold, 75 ; silver,
under the Bland-Allison
act, 109 ; gold, 173 ; silver,
177 ; currency, 187.
Charters of the national
banks, 57.
Chase, S. P., and the greenbacks, 127 ; and the na-
tional banks, 154.
Circulating medium, 2.
Circulation, tax on national
bank, 63 ; tax on govern-
ment note, 147, 192 ; outstanding national bank,
64.
Clearing-house certificates, 2.
Clearing-houses, origin and
purposes of, 68 ; methods
of, 170.
" Coin," construction by the
Treasury of the word, 20,
133.

Coinage act of 1873, 99.
Coinage system, development of the, 115.
Colfax, Speaker, and the ten per cent. bank tax, 158.
Committee legislation, 205.
Committees of Congress, control of finances by the, 22, 207.
Comptroller of the Currency, powers and duties of the, 32 ; reports of national banks to the, 62.
Congress, and the currency, 11, 207.
Conkling, Roscoe, and the legal-tender act, 146.
Constitution, implied powers under the, 190.
Convertibility of greenbacks into bonds, 156.
Currency, reports of the Secretary of the Treasury on the, 209.
Currency certificates at the clearing-houses, 76.
Customs dues, payment of, in coin, 82 ; payment of, in gold, 114.

Dallas, A. J., views of, on the power of Congress to regulate the currency, 7.
Debt, the public, and paper money, 83 ; the interest-bearing, of the United States, 84.
Decimal system, suggested by Jefferson, 116.
Demand notes, 149.
" Demonetization of silver, the," 103.
Depletion of the gold reserve, 94.
Deposits, the removal of the, by Jackson, 37 ; tax on national bank, 63.
Depositories, national banks as government, 58.
Dime, coinage of the, 118.
Director of the Mint, powers and duties of the, 36.
" Divorce of the government and the banks," 53, 228.
Dollar, coinage of the first silver, 118 ; coinage of the first gold, 118 ; the gold, made the standard, 102 ; intrinsic value of the silver, 102.
Double eagle, coinage of the, 121.
Dred Scott decision, the, and the legal-tender act, 116.

Eagle, coinage of the gold, 118.
Edmunds, Senator Geo. F., in the legal-tender cases, 198.
England, and the gold standard, 98 ; notes of the Bank of, 163.
Examiners, national bank, 62.
" Exchanges " at the clearing houses, 73.
Exportation of gold bullion, 114.
Extension act, national bank charter, 65.

Federalist view of the Constitution, the, 190.
Fessenden, Secretary, and the ten per cent. bank tax, 159, 203.
Field, Justice, dissenting opinion of, in the legal-tender cases, 199.
Financial policy of the United States, the, 15.

Fiscal year of the Treasury, 36.

Five per cent. redemption fund, the, 166.

Forced loan, the greenback a, 151.

Fractional currency, 148.

France, and the gold standard, 99.

" Free coinage," and the Bland-Allison act, 106 ; arguments in favor of, 114.

" Fugios," the first American coins, 26.

Gallatin, Secretary, and the clearing-houses, 77.

Garfield, James A., on the greenback, 139.

Gerry, Elbridge, and the Board of Treasury, 25.

Gold and silver, when unused as currency, 97.

" Gold banks," 169.

Gold certificates, clearing-house, 75 ; United States, 76.

Gold dollar, made the standard, 102.

Gold reserve, evils of the, 18 ; establishment of the, 21 ; bond issues to maintain the, 86 ; and business, 90 ; depletion of the, 94 ; expense of maintaining the, 95.

Gold standard, the, in Europe, 98.

Gordon, Wm. F., author of the Independent Treasury act, 41.

Grant, President, and the act of 1873, 101.

Greenback, the, where redeemable, 44 ; origin of, 125.

Greenback party, the, 144.

" Gresham's Law," operation of, in the United States, 97.

Half dollar, coinage of the, 118.

Half dime, coinage of the, 118.

Hamilton, Alexander, system of finance approved by, 4 ; " Report on a National Bank," by, 190.

" Hard money," in early financial history of the United States, 96.

Hepburn vs. *Griswold*, 194.

Hill, Senator David B., on the greenback, 146.

Jefferson's construction of the taxing power, 4 ; authorship of the Federal decimal system, 116.

Johnson, Justice, on federal control of the currency, 191.

Johnston, Prof. Alex., on the Sub-Treasury system, 54

Juilliard vs. *Greenman*, 197.

Knox, John J., Mint act of 1873, framed by, 100 ; on the silver certificate, 181.

Latin Union, the, and the gold standard, 99.

Legal-tender acts, the, 9, 126.

Legal-tender cases, the, 127, 195.

Limitation of bank-note circulation, 167.

Lincoln, and the national bank bill, 155.

Loan certificates of the New York Clearing-House, 78 ; liability of the, to the ten per cent. tax, 81.

Local taxation of banks, 161.
Lyman, Geo. D., first manager of the New •York Clearing-House, 78.

Mint act of 1873, 99.
Mint Bureau, a special division of the Treasury Department, 35.
Mint, establishment of the, 116 ; Director of the, 117 ; location of the, 118.
McCulloch, Hugh, plan of, to retire the greenbacks, 132 ; and the National bank act, 156.
McCulloch vs. *Maryland*, 195.
Morris, Robert, and the colonial finances, 24.

National Bank, Hamilton's " Report " on a, 4 ; method of organizing a, 56.
National Banks, number of, in the United States, 65.
National currency, an act to provide a, 153.
New York, clearing-house at, 77 ; Sub-Treasury at, a member of clearing-house, 81 ; Bank act of the State of, 160.
Nominal unit of value, 119.
Notes, amount of, issued by a national bank, 59; of national banks, subjects of state taxation, 63.

'Obligations," greenbacks judicially pronounced to be, 147, 193.
Osborne vs. *Bank of United States*, 191.

Paper, " distinctive," used for bank notes, 59.

Paper money, confused character of United States, 22 ; various kinds of, that have existed in the United States, 217.
Policy, statutory financial, of the United States, 184.
Postal currency, 148.
" Purchasing clause " of the Sherman act, 186.

Quarter dollar, coinage of the, 118.

Ratio, established by Mint act of 1792, 118 ; changed in 1834, 119.
Receivability of national bank notes, 162.
Re-charter of Bank of the United States, 5.
Redemption fund, the five per cent., 61 ; the national bank, 166.
Redemption of bank notes at the Treasury, 62 ; of Sherman act Treasury notes in gold and silver, 111 ; of State bank issues, 161.
Register of the Treasury, powers and duties of the, 34.
Re-issue of greenbacks made compulsory, 135 ; of Treasury notes and certificates, 186.
Repeal of the National Bank act attempted, 171.
Reports of the Secretary of the Treasury, 27 ; by the banks to the comptroller, 62 ; on the currency, 209.
Reserves and reserve cities, 64.
Résumé of the several kinds of currency, 214.

Resumption act, and the gold reserve, 91 ; purposes of the, 92 ; efforts to repeal the, 113 ; construction of word "coin," as used in the, 133.

Retirement of the greenbacks by McCulloch, 132.

Revisors of the United States Statutes, and legal tender silver, 105.

Rhode Island and the Constitutional Convention, 6.

Secretary of the Treasury, relation of Congress to the, 13, 28 ; duties and powers of the, 27.

Seigniorage under the Sherman act, 121.

Separation of the government from the banks, 48.

Sherman act, the, 183 ; passage of the, 110 ; silver bullion purchases under the, 113.

Sherman, John, advocates the legal-tender act, 147 ; introduces the national bank act, 155.

Silver dollar, always intrinsically the same, 102.

Silver, payment of, in settling clearing-house balances, 69 ; and gold, relative values of, prior to 1873, 97 ; amount of, purchased under the Sherman act, 120.

Spalding, E. G., author of the greenback legislation, 126.

Spanish silver dollar the continental standard, 116.

Specie payments, suspension of, 44.

Standard of value, 98 ; gold, in Europe, 98.

Standard silver dollars, number coined, 104.

State bank issues, tax on, 67, 158 ; volume of, 157.

Subsidiary silver, 123.

Sub-Treasury, scheme of the, devised by William F. Gordon, 41 ; advantages of the, 54.

Sub-Treasuries, number and location of, 43.

"Suffolk System, the," of State banks, 161.

Supreme Court decisions on currency, 190.

Taney, R. B., appointed Secretary of the Treasury to remove the deposits, 39.

Tax, on state bank issues, 201 ; on circulation of national banks, 63, 192 ; on deposits of national banks, 63 ; on United States notes and certificates, 192.

Taxation of currency by state governments, 147, 192.

Temporary purpose of the greenback, 153.

Three cent piece, coinage of the, 122.

Three dollar gold piece, coinage of the, 122.

"Token money," 103.

Trade dollar, origin and purpose of the, 122.

Treasurer of the United States, powers and duties of the, 31.

Treasury Department, origin of the, 24.

Treasury notes, not in vogue prior to 1862, 50 ; under the Sherman act, redeemed by Secretary Carlisle with silver, 112; ante-bellum, 129; or "greenbacks," issues of, 131.

Trenholm, W. I.., on the silver certificate and greenbacks, 164.

Twenty cent piece, coinage of the, 123.

Upton, J. K., on the currency certificates, 189.

Uses of the Sub-Treasury under existing statutes, 226.

Veazie Bank vs. *Fenno*, 201.

Virginia the first colony to make the Spanish dollar the standard, 116.

Ways and Means, greenback legislation originated with Committee of the, 126.

Windom, Secretary, coinage scheme proposed by, 183.

www.ingramcontent.com/pod-product-compliance
Lightning Source LLC
Chambersburg PA
CBHW020102030726
47498CB00006B/1911